# THE STORY OF HOPE:

## The Nation,
## The Man,
## The Kingdom

Ronald A. Sarno, S.J.

LIGUORI PUBLICATIONS
Liguori, Missouri 63057

Imprimi Potest:
Robert A. Mitchell, S.J.
Provincial, New York Province
Society of Jesus
July 1, 1971


Imprimatur:
St. Louis, March 14, 1972
+ Charles R. Koester
Vicar General of St. Louis

Library of Congress Catalog Card Number: 72-075145

**THIS BOOK
IS
DEDICATED:**

To all who have shared their lives with me.
To older friends who gave me a heritage
worth preserving.
To younger friends who offer me a future
worth working for.

# ACKNOWLEDGEMENTS

This book popularizes the current theology of hope. It will employ the findings of several contemporary Scripture scholars. Their insights have helped the author to organize his material. He has tried meticulously to cite his sources for those who wish to pursue the subject more deeply.

Class presentations at Woodstock and at Union Theological have helped the author of this text to arrange his material more carefully. When using a professor's particular organization of the material, the author considers it only fair to give him credit for the assistance. However, these citations are used for the particular viewpoint of this book, and it would be unfair to attribute them to the teachers cited. All of them are better scholars at theology than I am, and they should not be held responsible for my opinions.

A special thanks should be given to Father Richard Dillon, Father Robert O'Brien, S.J., Father Edward Mally, S.J., and Professor George Landes. Their classes and encouragement were a real inspiration for this work.

Citations from Scripture and Vatican II are indented. The quotes from Scripture employ the translation of *The Jerusalem Bible* (ed. Alexander Jones, Garden City, N.Y.: Doubleday, 1966). At certain times the author uses his own translation of the original Biblical languages. These are noted whenever they occur. The quotations from Vatican II are from the translation of *The Documents of Vatican II* (ed. Walter M. Abbott, S.J., New York: America Press, 1966).

Much of the theology of hope is "in the air." Therefore, the author might inadvertently have missed crediting the proper scholar in certain places.

# ABBREVIATIONS USED IN THIS TEXT

| | |
|------|------|
| D | Deuteronomist |
| E | Elohist |
| ed. | editor |
| ET | English Translation |
| J | Yahwist |
| JBC | The Jerome Biblical Commentary |
| JE | An early conflation of J and E |
| LXX | The Septuagint, the Greek version of the Old Testament |
| MT | The Massoretic Text, the Hebrew Old Testament |
| n. | footnote |
| no. | paragraph number |
| NT | New Testament |
| P | Priestly Tradition |
| Q | *The Sayings of Jesus*, collections of Jesus' sayings which predate the Gospels |
| trans. | translator |

# CONTENTS

# INTRODUCTION

## The Theology of Hope

Ernst Bloch's *The Principles of Hope* first appeared in German in 1959.[1] Written by a humanist and a socialist, the book explored the philosophical basis for man's hope to change the future of his world. Jürgen Moltmann, professor of systematic theology at the University of Tübingen, employed these philosophical principles to formulate his own Christian theology.[2] His theology of hope sets the foundations for a new Christian identity. The Christian is no longer someone who passively assents to intellectual propositions which have been handed down to him as the deposit of faith. Now the Christian sees himself as a man of hope, actively co-working with the Father and His Son Jesus Christ to remake the world in His image.

*Theology of Hope* caused an avalanche of books, articles, and lectures on the subject of Christian hope. Obviously, this theology is not an ivy-tower system remote from the real needs of Christians. The articulation of this theology strikes a responsive chord immediately. Clearly, the theology of hope gives the intellectual foundation for what the modern Christians personally accept as their role in the world: a people of hope, men and women, who earnestly wish to prepare the world for the kingdom of God.

This book wishes to explore the new self-iden-

---

[1]Das Prinzip Hoffnung (Frankfurt: Suhrkamp, 1959).

[2]*Theology of Hope,* trans. James W. Leitch (New York: Harper and Row, 1967). Hereafter cited as: Moltmann.

tity. It has to do not so much with theology as with a community of people who have identified themselves as a people of hope. This community bases its new identity as a people of hope on their historical continuity with the men and women who have been an active part of salvation history.

The book hopes to show how the major figures in salvation history really were men of hope. Thus, we will regard Israel as a nation of hope. We will treat of Jesus Christ as a Man of hope. We will explore the Christian community as a people of hope.

Certain elements of salvation hope will occur throughout the book. Perhaps it would be helpful to note them at once. These are the traits which men of hope have shared throughout all of salvation history. Surely we expect them in the future.

1) *The Divine Invitation:* In the depths of his own personal self-consciousness, the recipient realizes that God is summoning him to cooperate with Him in salvation history. He is asked to communicate this invitation to others, who must make an act of faith in the divine commission.

2) *Trust and Confidence:* His own faith is now a personal trust and confidence that God will help him as he tries to bring others to work with him. He clings to this belief in spite of all opposition.

3) *Personal Courage:* In spite of every human reason to desist he continues this task even when failure seems certain. He is more confident in God than in any form of "reasonable behavior."

4) *The Future:* He does not abandon the present; he works very hard at making the present ready for God. But no matter what the present may do to deny his call as divine, he is certain that the future will justify his current behavior. The future will show the legitimacy of his claim to be doing God's work on earth.

# A EUCHARISTIC PRAYER
# FOR THE PEOPLE OF HOPE

Perhaps the following prayer will let our readers know in what spirit we write. The text is based on an experimental Eucharistic prayer shown to me by Father Thomas Dunn, O.F.M., and Father Gary Schwartzkopf, S.J.

**People:** Eternal Father, You are the source of all that is true and good among men. We thank You for the human gifts of life, love and friendship. We come together as a community to celebrate the goodness and beauty which You have given us. We will share the bread and cup on this table as a sign of the unity we already possess and as a pledge of what we hope to enjoy together in the future. We thank You for the beauty which we have already seen, for wonders yet to come, and for the persons whom we love, who by sharing themselves with us, give our lives meaning and direction.

We praise the men and women of courage who have gone before us. Their love and dedication overwhelmed those who would fall victim to darkness and despair. We praise the goodness of persons of all races, cultures, and religions — all who have stood up to repression and spent their lives in liberating their fellow-men. Through their humanity and dedication, our world has become more a place of hope.

Into our world of darkness they brought Your light. Into our world of coldness and indifference, they brought Your warmth and acceptance. Into our world of sin and despair, they brought Your forgiveness and hope. When we grew eager for war, they brought peace. When we blindly suffocated others with injustice and oppression, they proclaimed liberation and hope.

As people of all times and in all places have praised You under different names and in diverse ways, so now we express our admiration and gratitude. Conscious of our own place in salvation history we thank You for the just rulers, holy priests, and brave prophets whom You sent to Israel. Among all of those who brought hope to our world, one man stands out for us who call ourselves Christians. So we especially praise You for Your Son, Jesus Christ. He chose to come to us as a Man of hope who brought light and healing to our world.

We thank You for Jesus Christ, who was a restless Man, and a Man of justice, who would not accept our world as it was, but preached to us the mystery of Your coming into human history: "The kingdom of God is at hand; repent and believe the Gospel." He preached a kingdom of justice and love, and challenged all of us who would grow satisfied with our world to become a free people, men and women who would take hold of our own lives and of our world, throw down the oppression of fear and loneliness, and stand strong and free in His kingdom of life.

Because He preached human liberation He was arrested and tried, found guilty and crucified, the victim of our weak fear and despair. But You raised Him up again, the first-born of Your new kingdom, the eldest of many brothers and sisters. You set Him over all creation, and through His victory we have become free men, unafraid of failure and death. Therefore we praise You for Your eternal freedom and power and majesty.

We are grateful for this unforgettable Man, who has fulfilled everything that is human. We thank You, because He gave himself, heart and soul, to our world.

Celebrant: And on the evening when one of His friends fell victim to despair, abandoned His message of hope, and preferred the lonely night rather than join Him in His last meal, He took bread, gave thanks to You, broke it, and distributed it among His companions, saying: *This is My body broken for you. Every time you share this bread, you share it with Me.*

Then He took the cup filled with wine, and giving thanks to You, said: *This is the new covenant of My blood, shed for you, and for all men. Every time you share this cup, you remember what I have done for you.*

Together let us proclaim the mystery of our faith:

**People:** Your holy death, O Lord, we remember.
Your glorious Resurrection we proclaim.
Your coming in glory we await in hope.

We pray that we may go forward in life, ready to bear with others and to pardon each other. We wish to be open and accepting, respectful of every person we meet. May we always be faithful to our friends who rely on us. We pray that we may work ceaselessly to prepare our world for Your coming kingdom, the new earth, which surpasses all our dreams and aspirations. Help us to face disappointments and never lose heart.

Guide our spiritual and civic leaders in Your way. We pray that in the midst of this world, we may be a people of hope, a sign of Your peace, that we may support and serve each other in love, that our hearts may be open to Your Spirit who urges us on to respond to the poor, the sick, those disillusioned by life, those who are broken in any way. Call people from among us to combat poverty and hopelessness. Enable us to find a way to end hunger and to stop the wars in our world.

We are sustained by your power, Father, which transcends us, and so we are bold enough, in the face of all the signs which contradict Your presence in our world, to look forward in hope to that day when all mankind can live together in a genuine community of justice, love, and peace.

Through Jesus Christ, who lives and reigns with You, together with the Holy Spirit, now, and in the kingdom to come. Amen.

# Part I:

# ISRAEL:
# THE NATION OF HOPE

At all times and among every people, God has given welcome to whosoever fears Him and does what is right. It has pleased God, however, to make men holy and save them not merely as individuals without any mutual bonds, but by making them into a single people, a people which acknowledges Him in truth and serves Him in holiness. He therefore chose the race of Israel as a people unto himself. With it He set up a covenant. Step by step He taught this people by manifesting in its history both himself and the decrees of His will, and by making it holy unto himself (*Constitution on the Church*, no. 9).

## The Summons to Freedom

Israel traced her origins back to a community of slaves oppressed by the Pharaoh of Egypt. As a nation, they had preferred security rather than risk. They had abandoned any hope of changing their role in history. They had accepted despair and regarded themselves as unable to have any control over their future. Fat and comfortable, they forgot the promises made to the patriarchs.

Why and how did a group of slaves become a people? Israel's language indicates that it was aware of the fact that its historical liberation was not the outcome of its vocation for freedom. They were not committed to a vocation to be free. On the contrary, the fleshpots of Egypt were more attractive than the far away hope for a land of freedom. They would rather survive in bondage than die on the way to a new tomorrow. This was the protest continuously heard during the journey through the desert. From an alalysis of their consciousness one could not envisage any possibility of liberation. The objective ways seemed equally blocked. The yoke of slavery was heavy. The oppressor was militarily strong. And they, the slaves, were weak, with no weapons, with no discipline, no determination. The political power of Egypt, the unsurmountable obstacles of the journey, the survival in the desert, the problem of the conquest of the land — all these elements of the situation pointed in the same direction: the future was closed.

The people of Israel, consequently, could not see their liberation either as the result of their determination to be free or as having been made possible by the circumstances. They had not made themselves free: they were forced to be free.[1]

God himself was the one who would not permit them to be enslaved, secure, comfortable, or satisfied. He summoned them to freedom, a freedom which they did not particularly want but which He wanted for His own people. He was the God of risk, of promise, of liberation. He offered them a future

---

[1]Rubem A. Alves, *A Theology of Human Hope* (Washington: Corpus, 1969), p. 89. Hereafter cited as Alves.

with Him. He virtually changed them from a colony of slaves, a colony of despair, into a nation, a nation of hope.

He was not a God of remote transcendence, but one who acted within history, forcing history to do His will. But He sought the cooperation of men, for He summoned certain individuals to be His charismatic leaders. He was thus a God of promise, of inspired leaders, of historical events.

Each event made Israel into a free people. The ancient Israelites, when they talked or wrote about God, recited a story, a story of God's activity among men. Each retelling strengthened their hope that God would be with them in the present and the future, because He had manifested himself to His nation in the past.

One of the oldest prayers recorded in the Old Testament is a thanksgiving recital to be said when offering God gratitude for the first-fruits of the harvest. Gratitude for the present bounty is expressed by recalling the events of salvation history. This is not done to sacralize the past, but to lay the ground for hope in the future (Alves, p. 91).

My father was a wandering Aramean. He went down into Egypt to find refuge there, few in numbers; but there he became a nation, great, mighty, and strong. The Egyptians ill-treated us, they gave us no peace and inflicted harsh slavery on us. But we called on Yahweh the God of our fathers. Yahweh heard our voice and saw our misery, our toil and our oppression; and Yahweh brought us out of Egypt with mighty hand and outstretched arm, with great terror, and with signs and wonders. He brought us here and gave us this land, a land where milk and honey flow (Dt. 26:5-9).

# A Chronology of the Major Events in Israel's History

**Dates:**

| | |
|---|---|
| 2000 B.C. – 1300 B.C | The ancestors of Israel are nomadic shepherds in the Near East and Egypt. 1850: Abraham in Canaan. 1700: Patriarchs in Egypt. |
| 1300 B.C. – 1200 B.C. | Exodus, Moses, the Law at Sinai, Joshua invades Palestine. |
| 1200 B.C. – 1000 B.C. | Tribal confederation united by a common worship of Yahweh. Local government, worship at tribal shrines. |
| 1000 B.C. – 587 B.C. | Monarchy. Centralized government and centralized worship at Jerusalem. Saul: 1030-1010; David: 1010-970; Solomon: 970-931. In 931 the Northern Kingdom, Israel, secedes from Judah. Israel falls in 721; Judah in 587. |
| 587 B.C. – 538 A.D. | Babylonian Exile |
| 538 B.C. – 70 A.D. | Restoration. The Jews ruled by the Persians, the Hellenists, and the Romans. Jerusalem destroyed by Titus and the Romans in 70 A.D. |

## The National Consciousness

Israel's contemporaries formed their national consciousness out of myth. Israel made a radical break with such a consciousness. Israel did not consider itself mythically. Rather, the nation learned about God and experienced His activity within history and not outside of it. Also, Israel did not view itself as isolated from the other nations around it. Rather, the nation viewed itself as a genuine part of the world community. In Gen. 10-11, Israel deliberately lists itself within the table of nations of the world. The nation of hope lives within time and within the community of men.[2]

The nation Israel was united by mutual religious faith. But Israel did not see this as an intellectual act. They did not all share a universal intellectual assent to the same theological propositions. Rather, their national unity came from a shared hope. True Israelites shared an abiding confidence that God had kept His promises in the past and would continue to guide them in their historical destiny.

I, for my part, like an olive tree
   growing in the house of God,
   put my trust in God's love
   for ever and ever.

I mean to thank you constantly
   for doing what you did,
and put my hope in your name,
      that is so full of kindness,
   in the presence of those who love you (Ps. 52:
   8-9).

"Belief (faith) is 'fixing oneself on Yahweh' and refers as a rule to God's future saving act. Belief is

---

[2]Gerhard von Rad, *Genesis: A Commentary,* trans. John Marks (Philadelphia: Westminster Press, 1961), p. 141. Hereafter cited as: von Rad.

an act of trust, a consent to God's plan in history" (von Rad, p. 142).

Such a hope also demands that the people place their trust in God's chosen representative. He could reveal to them what God expected of them in the future. "The events of the future lay in Yahweh's hand only, and only the one to whom it was revealed was empowered to interpret" (von Rad, p. 366). The man of hope, so graced by God, did not always receive a universal welcome. For invariably he challenged the present conditions and forced the people to come to terms with their future. They must choose God over and above their own comfort. Often the prophet's life was in danger, for he proclaimed the will of God and once again demanded risk, danger, and death for the sake of the future. The present was always, to Israel, more real than the future, comfort more satisfying than hope. "This was the reason the prophets were so violently persecuted, because the effectiveness and validity of their words were indissolubly connected with their personal existence" (von Rad, p. 348).

For Israel, history did not mean the reporting of chronological events. Rather, history meant drama. Yahweh called out to His people through His charismatic leaders. Would the people accept such leadership or turn away? Moses was accepted, and the people gained a whole new future: nationhood. Jeremiah was rejected, and the people lost their future to the conquering pagans. Thus, none of the books of the Old Testament is really scientific history, but rather they are accounts of salvation history, of whether the nation responded to God's message of hope or preferred to stay in the present.

There is another history that a people make besides the externals of wars, victories, migrations, and political catastrophes. It is an inner history, one that takes place on a higher level, a story of inner events, experiences, and singular guidance, or working and becoming mature in life's mysteries; to put it simply, a history with God. And even though it is certainly not to be asserted that this history does not have a close connection with the former, nevertheless it is not at all the same; and, above all, the manner of its representation and visualization is different (von Rad, p. 32).

Such a representation could be done by a faith-story, which will be discussed more fully below. Throughout the nation's history, the sacred writings of the Old Testament were gradually accumulated from oral and literary traditions which met a specific need of the people at a certain time. The Yahwist, for instance, strove to demonstrate that God had remained with His people, after the Davidic monarchy had ended the familiar tribal government and local cultic worship (von Rad, p. 176).

The Elohist traditions of the Pentateuch, which set out to provide definite religious teaching, reminded Israel of the fact that it was chosen by God to be His own people. Deuteronomy and the Deuteronomic history (Joshua, Judges, Samuel and Kings) depict Israel's faithlessness, show that this was bound to lead to catastrophe, and in this way exhort the rest of God's people to conversion and penance. The particular tradition of the Pentateuch, which is designated by the letter *P* [priestly], means to set out a program of spiritual restoration after the exile, based on the old traditions. The prophets attribute Israel's lack of loyalty to its old traditions and summon the people to a searching of heart and penance. It is true that the psalms did not originate as popular songs, but they were certainly intended for participation by all the people in the form of one chorus or alternating choruses. The wisdom literature, particularly Proverbs and Sirach (Ecclesiasticus), is again more deeply rooted in popular tradition. It is less directly concerned with a definite religious message for Israel, but shows very clearly that the world and the ordinary reality of everyday life have a definite place in the religious experience of Israel.[3]

(These four sources will be explained more fully later in this book.)

For the nation had begun with God, and since He remained faithful to His pledge, the nation still hoped in His divine guidance, even when every human reason cried against such an assertion.

Israel believed that it began as a nation with God's promise to certain men and their hope in His fidelity. God invited them to share in salvation history and these individuals made this salvation a reality within the nation by their personal response to God's summons. Therefore, the basic thematic thread which runs throughout the first six books of the Old Testament (Genesis, Exodus, Leviticus, Numbers, Deuteronomy, and Joshua) is: God, who made the world as a gift for man, personally summoned the patriarchs to trust in Him. He promised them the land of Canaan as a pledge of His fidelity to this promise. When Israel became a mighty host in the land of Egypt, He chose Moses to lead His people out of bondage. He favored them with special signs and wonders to protect them on the journey. Finally, under Joshua, He gave them the Promised Land (von Rad, pp. 13-14).

The Scriptural accounts of the story knit together the old oral traditions about the patriarchs

---

[3]Bastiaan Van Iersel, S.M.M. "The Book of the People of God," *The Human Reality of Sacred Scripture* Vol. X Concilium Series (New York: Paulist, 1965), p. 30.

by constantly repeating the central theme: the promise of land (von Rad, p. 21). God summons each of the patriarchs to hope in His plan to fulfill that promise. They are given no indication of *how* God will do it. They are simply asked to make an act of trust in His ability to *do* it. So each patriarch sojourns throughout the Promised Land; he sees the Canaanites enjoying his birthright; he remains completely powerless to change his role as a landless and weak wanderer; yet he hopes in that future time when God would be true to His promise.

This promise belonged to the nation as a whole, and not only to an individual Israelite. Even after the land of Canaan had been completely conquered (by David, who finally subjected the pagan cities to Israelite control), the promise still remained. The nation still hoped in God's promise, for His fidelity had now been proven. God and Israel still had a mutual future. Each Israelite saw himself intimately linked with his ancestors and descendants. He was assumed by a "great living organism with a common destiny" (von Rad, p. 397). Each Israelite personally participated in the whole history of the nation. He actively shared in the hope of the patriarchs. He marched toward freedom with the armies of the Exodus. He too fought to secure the conquest of the Holy Land. He lived with the promise made to the patriarchs: it was his hope, too. He shared in the nation's glorious future. So, for a very long time, an Israelite could dispense with any specific hope for a personal existence after death. He was one with the nation of hope. The nation survived, for God had guaranteed its future. He shared most intimately in that future. He did not need a personal future beyond death, for he already was a living part of the nation which had been promised a share in God's future. He already possessed a destiny beyond death (von Rad, p. 397).

After the exile Israel's national institutions, the Davidic monarchy and the Aaronite priesthood, failed the people. Then the Jews came to realize that their own future would not be a solitary benefit for themselves, but would become a source of salvation for all of the people of the world. Their nation of hope would beacon God's salvation to all men. The Messianic king would usher in this new role for the nation.

> The scepter shall not pass from Judah,
> nor the mace from between his feet,
> until he comes to whom it belongs,
> to whom the peoples shall render obedience (Gen. 49:10).

This Messianic oracle comes from Jacob's blessing to his son Judah as recorded at the end of Genesis. Although the saying could be applied to King David, it seems to be a definite Messianic prediction. It foretells that the kingdom of Judah would last "until" a ruler came who would reign over all of the peoples, not only the Israelites. Further, the rest of the saying predicts the restoration of the fruitfulness of Paradise, a theme often associated with the coming of the Messianic kingdom (von Rad, p. 420).

## The Faith-Story

Scientific history records past events in their precise chronological sequence. The past remains remote, even though it brought about the present environment of the narrator who now writes about it. On the other hand, the faith-story does not separate past events of salvation history from the narrator's present environment. The faith-story tells of an historical experience of his community which lives on in the present. He writes about a faith, not of a past faith, but one which he is now practicing (von Rad, p. 33). He retells the faith-story precisely as a guide for the community in which he now lives;

he also hopes that his narrative will serve as a guide for future believers. The narrator of the faith-story makes an act of hope in the future of his own faith.

Each faith-story centers on a charismatic leader whose own life sums up the basic historical experience which originally belonged to the community as a whole and not just to one man. In other words, the narrative of the leader's life is used as a summary for the events which happened to the whole nation. Such a practice, which disturbs our modern scientific bent, stems from the oral traditions which were the origin of these stories. For oral primitive people, lacking the written word, use such a device to preserve their own history. Each faith-story in the Old Testament is about a man of hope, and his life sums up the hope which guided the nation in the past and would continue to guide it in the future. Israel preserved this tradition by relating faith-stories about its charismatic leaders.

In oral cultures virtually all conceptualization, including what will later be reshaped into abstract sciences, is thus kept close to the human life-world. Moreover, since public law and custom are of major importance for social survival but cannot be put on record, they must constantly be talked about or sung about, else they vanish from consciousness. Hence the figures around whom knowledge is made to cluster, those about whom stories are told or sung, must be made into conspicuous personages, focuses of common attention, individuals embodying open public concerns, as written laws would later be matters of open public concern. In other words, the figures around whom knowledge is made to cluster must be heroes, culturally 'large' or 'heavy' figures like Odysseus or Achilles or Oedipus.[4]

---

[4] Walter Ong, S.J. *The Presence of the Word* (New Haven: Yale, 1967), p. 204. Hereafter cited as: Ong.

The pagan myths deliberately transfigured and idealized such heroes into something more than human stature. However, the Old Testament faith-story completely dispenses with such idealization of its central character. The narrator of the faith-story carefully portrays the patriarchs and Moses with sober realism. The faith-story records both their human greatness, and painstakingly, their weakness of character also. The men who led their nation had to come to terms with their own weakness, sin and failure (von Rad, p. 34). The faith-story is not a hagiography encouraging imitation of its protagonist. Rather, it is much more concerned about God and how He acts with men than with the men themselves. There is no attempt to glorify them.

Noah drank too much wine; Jacob cheated his brother Esau out of his father's blessing; Moses killed an Egyptian in the heat of anger. These men are never important in the faith-story for their own sakes, but rather in how they respond to God as a person who can both affirm and deny God and his command (von Rad, p. 35). God summoned each of them to hope in his promise, and all of them heeded this summons. Such men therefore become symbols of a universal religious truth (von Rad, p. 39).

Such a religious truth can be expressed as follows: God cannot bring hope to men unless His chosen representatives respond to His call. The ground of hope always remains the individual's personal response to God's request that he cooperate with Him in the work of salvation. Each faith-story aims its narrative directly at the heart of the present community. It does not encourage drunkenness, cheating or murder, but it forces everyone to realize that even men subject to such weaknesses can bring God's hope to earth. Once they assent to God's summons, they become men of hope; their sin shrinks into insignificance because they have had the personal greatness to say "Yes!" to God.

## The Four Sources

The faith-stories of the Pentateuch began with the oral tales which were recited by the ancient Israelites. Later collectors assembled these stories, edited them for their own purposes, and wrote them down to meet a specific need of their own community. The present text, therefore, consists of a conscious editorial conflation of these separate written accounts. The four major written sources for the early books of the Bible are: the Yahwist (J), the Elohist (E), the Priestly (P), and the Deuteronomist (D). An early editor combined the J and E traditions, and this is called JE.

J comes from a ninth century B.C. Judean source favorable to the Davidic monarchy. E is an eighth century B.C. work from the Northern Kingdom. P was done by many generations of Jerusalem priests after the exile. D comes from Judah during the seventh century B.C. when Josiah had initiated his reforms.[5]

The J narrative possesses a colorful style and a personal tone. J refers to God directly by His personal name, Yahweh. It portrays God anthropomorphically. He speaks directly to men; He walks with them in the cool of the evening. On the other hand, E preserves a more reverent tradition. It refers to God as Elohim, the Hebrew word for God. It rarely mentions His personal name Yahweh, and God does not speak directly to men, but employs a mediator. Sometimes this is the angel of Yahweh; at other times it is a dream. E does not portray man in

---

[5]Eugene Maly, "Introduction to the Pentateuch," *Jerome Biblical Commentary I* (Englewood Cliffs, N.J.: Prentice Hall, 1968), p. 2, no. 8. Hereafter cited as: *JBC.*

immediate contact with God as J does. This loss of personal immediacy with God and His word of summons puts a new emphasis on the role of the prophet. He becomes the chosen mediator between God and men. He receives God's message to bring the promise of hope to his people. He also brings men's petitions back to God (von Rad, p. 25).

E, therefore, probably derives from the circle of prophets in Israel. This particular prophetic tradition, however, comes from a time when these prophets sympathized with the sanctuary and the official cult. The later major prophets often attacked the official cult as a meaningless formalism (von Rad, p. 223).

JE records secular events. God works in hidden ways through profane history. It encourages Israelites to continue to trust in God's promises. He is still guiding His people to their mutual future with Him. In the past, He chose dramatic sacred events to demonstrate His concern. Now He chooses to work through the events of human history. P, on the other hand, tells about the specific revelation of God in sacred history. It narrates about events which are definitively sacred in character (von Rad, p. 333).

P is replete with geneologies, cultic and liturgical legislation. The tradition emphasizes what comes from God to men: "His words, judgments, commands, and regulations" (von Rad, p. 26).

P stresses the notion of the pilgrim people. The true Israelite is always on a journey to a new future with God. He cannot rest in the Promised Land, but must seek anew what God is calling him to do. The P narrative of Jacob's visit to Pharaoh in Egypt underscores this theme:

> Pharaoh asked Jacob, 'How many years of life can you reckon?' 'My life of wandering has lasted one hundred and thirty years,' Jacob told Phar-

aoh, 'few years and unhappy, falling short of the years of my fathers in their life of wandering' (Gen. 47:8-9).

In P, the patriarchs "wander" throughout the Holy Land. The term "wandering" implies a renunciation of settlement and ownership. It means a life oriented toward the future, toward the promise of land which was often renewed to the patriarchs. So each patriarch lived with a curious ambiguous relationship to promise and fulfillment — in the Holy Land. Here the "life of wandering" took place (von Rad, p. 402-3). They could hope only in a promised future yet to come. They had no joy of possession; they could not settle. They kept on the move, always uncomfortable. They lived in risk, their only security being their hope that God would be faithful to His promise.

## The Theology of the Yahwist

The Davidic monarchy had centralized Israel's government at Jerusalem, the old pagan city which had belonged to the Jebusites during the time of the judges (1200-1000 B.C.). The worship of Yahweh, which had been performed at local shrines by tribal patriarchs, now moved to the central sanctuary in the city of David. Temple priests took over the sacrifices once done by the patriarchs. Many Israelites felt uneasy about these sweeping changes. Despair crept into their lives; they felt that they had lost their historical link with God. Had He not ordained their patriarchial worship and their tribal government? Did they not abandon their traditional trust in God by relying on the power of the Jerusalem hegemony? (von Rad, p. 176).

'So give us a king to rule over us, like the other nations.' It displeased Samuel that they should say, 'Let us have a king to rule us,' so he prayed to Yahweh. But Yahweh said to Samuel,

'Obey the voice of the people in all that they say to you, for it is not you they have rejected; they have rejected me from ruling over them' (I Sam. 8:5-7).

The Yahwist insists that God stayed faithful to His people throughout all of these changes. He remained faithful to His promise. The new form of government and the new place of worship did not destroy the nation of hope. Instead, it offered it a new future.

J views the Davidic monarchy and the temple cult as the fulfillment of the promises made to the patriarchs. J did not see Jerusalem's political and religious hegemony as a national apostasy from God. By striving to unravel God's continuing care for His people, J laid the foundation for the basic theme of the Pentateuch and Joshua: the promise of God to the patriarchs, and the complete conquest of Palestine as the fulfillment of that ancient hope (von Rad, p. 22).

In J God makes the promise to Abraham and the hope is renewed with each patriarch:

God tells Abraham:

'Look all around from where you are towards the north and the south, towards the east and the west. All the land within sight I will give to you and your descendents for ever. I will make your descendents like the dust on the ground: when men succeed in counting the specks of dust on the ground, then they will be able to count your descendants!' (Gen. 13:14-16)

He offers the same hope to Isaac:

'I am the God of your father Abraham.

Do not be afraid, for I am with you.

I will bless you and make your descendants many in number

on account of my servant Abraham' (Gen. 26:24).

He repeats it to Jacob:

'I am Yahweh, the God of Abraham your father, and the God of Isaac. I will give to you and your descendants the land on which you are lying. Your descendants shall be like the specks of dust on the ground; you shall spread to the west and the east, to the north and the south, and all the tribes of the earth shall bless themselves by you and your descendants' (Gen. 28:13-14).

Nothing less than each man's personal cooperation could make this divine promise come true. If each individual did not truly hope in this promise, it became meaningless. Why? Once he personally accepted it, trusted in it, and lived his own life to make it a reality, then the hope grew with relentless vigor. The Yahwist's theology relied heavily on the need for human cooperation. In this way he goes far beyond the accepted notions of his day. His contemporaries believed that God's activity among men was limited to the sacred institutions, specifically the tribal government and the patriarchial worship. J accepts the belief that God worked through these sacred institutions in the past but he also sees God working in the quiet of the human heart as well as in the great sweeps of historical change. He believes that God works in the inner tabernacle of each man's conscience where the latter must wrestle alone with the divine invitation to cooperate with the work of grace. Thus God operates not only in the sacred, but also in the profane. His work appears in wondrous miracles, but also in the depths of man's heart. In the faith-story of Jacob and that of Joseph the reader almost feels that J conceives that God even works in and through human sin! (von Rad, p. 28)

J's theology concentrates on the mystery of man. What goes on in his heart? How does he respond to that unique summons from God? He (that is J) explores the great riddle of man: his visible behavior, his mistakes, and the conflicts within his heart. Among the Biblical writers, he stands out as the great psychologist. In a sense, he is an existentialist who depicts man acting in the real world. Still his view does not portray man as someone who in his despair conceives of himself as living alone in the universe. Rather he writes about man in relation; he describes man in a personal relationship with the living God. God reveals himself and His will to man. In J, man becomes the recipient of the divine dialogue. He is asked to respond. He becomes the recipient of the divine activity; he is asked to cooperate. The person so treated is summoned to hope in God's promise and to cooperate in the work of salvation history. Such a request puts him in an immediate and terrifying tension: he is now subject to divine salvation and divine judgment (von Rad, p. 24).

J's contemporaries felt that God had withdrawn himself from human history. The nation no longer possessed those sacred institutions in which they had encountered Him in the past. In contrast, J claimed that this was not true. In the past Yahweh had manifested himself in the glorious holy wars. Now God worked in concealed ways, in the course of profane history. J rejoiced to find God working so with His people in His hidden guidance of secular history, for this affirmed his own tenacious faith that God continued His personal care of the nation (von Rad, pp. 29-30). Such a belief formed a true ground for the nation of hope. They could go forward in confidence to their new future with God.

What exactly would this new future be for Israel?

We can understand the answer to this question better by studying precisely what new thrust J added to the traditional material which he had inherited from the older tribal theology. The tribal tradition about the conquest began with the faith-stories about the patriarchs. These conquest narratives did not include the cycle of primitive history (Adam, Abel, Noah, and the Tower of Babel). J yoked these primitive stories together with the patriarchial stories of salvation history. Since the tribal tradition had not included the primitive material, J could use it to develop his own theological conception. Actually, we do not possess any strict documentary evidence that J was really the first theologian to combine primitive history and salvation history. Yet there is also no evidence that J had access to any accepted tradition of this combination. The union strikes the reader as a bold, new concept (von Rad, p. 22).

J gathered his material on primitive history from many different sources. He used these stories to insist that all the corruption, despair, and confusion in the world comes only from one source: sin. The refusal to respond to God's gracious invitation has brought about all of man's sorrows. His primitive history depicts a continually widening gulf between God and man. Yet J has a paradoxical note of hope, for as the condition between God and mankind worsens, it is accompanied by the increasing power of grace working in secret within man (von Rad, p. 22).

J's stories about the fall, Cain, and Noah testify that God forgives men and supports them with His salvation (von Rad, pp. 22-23). J's primitive history draws to a close with the story of the Tower of Babel. The judgment of God appears as almost His final renunciation of any cooperation with men. But before despair can set in, He offers a new hope to man. God initiates salvation history with His summons to Abraham. He calls Abraham from out of the multitude of nations so that in him "all the nations shall be blessed."

Yahweh said to Abram, 'Leave your country, your family, and your father's house, for the land I will show you. I will make you a great nation; I will bless you and make your name so famous that it will be used as a blessing.

I will bless those who bless you:

I will curse those who slight you.

All the tribes of the earth

shall bless themselves by you'[6] (Gen. 12:1-3).

For J primitive history leaves mankind with the great question mark of despair: has God utterly abandoned men? His insertion of salvation history into his account of primitive history at this moment comforts man with the divine answer, hope. God has not left man, but selected one man for His very own. The disturbing question of primitive history (and the one foremost in the minds of J's contemporaries) remained: how did God relate to men? The answer of salvation history is: God relates to men through His chosen representatives. He has selected His own people for this relationship with men, and this people descends from Abraham. Genesis 12:1-3 not only initiates salvation history. For J it contains the joyful conclusion of primitive history too, for God calls Abraham out of the multitudes of the people of the world. He does not separate him from them, but makes him a source of God's blessing for them.

---

[6]For verse 3, MT reads $w^e nivr^e ku$, the niphal of *brk,* "to bless." The niphal can either be reflexive or passive; for *brk,* the niphal is most often reflexive, hence the correct translation would be: "shall bless themselves by you" which would mean "may you be as blest as Abraham!" LXX and MT translate the term passively: "in you all the nations shall be blessed." This second interpretation cannot be ruled out completely for J's own understanding of the role of Abraham in salvation history. The first would be a more exclusively nationalistic interpretation; the second a more universal one.

Abraham's summons reveals the key to the mystery of primitive history. God remains with men through His chosen ones. With this divine summons to Abraham, J shows his contemporaries the answer to their own dilemma. He shows them the link between their tribal past and their new monarchial situation. He shows them the union between the sacred and the profane, and the relationship of Israel to the world around it. He reveals Israel's new future: to be a sign and source of salvation for all men. Israel is to bring God's salvation to men.

This is the new future for Israel hidden within its own profane history. The Holy Land has now been totally subjugated. The promises of the past have met their own future and become the present. Now a new future must open up for God's people. Now Yahweh summons the nation to bridge the chasm between God and all of mankind. J does not demonstrate this new role with arguments from reason. He does not make it understandable by spelling out all of the implications which it involved.

He too remained unsure of how God would work out this new future for the nation. He simply announced it. He told Israel it must march forward to its new future. As in the past, the nation had to retain its confidence and trust in God. J expected Israel to continue to rely on God's control over history.

Gen. 12:1-3 offered Abraham three promises: 1) Abraham will be blessed and become a great nation. For J's generation this had come true. 2) Yahweh would give the land to Abraham's descendants. God had also fulfilled this promise for J's contemporaries. 3) In Abraham all of the tribes of the world would bless themselves. This has yet to come true. Here J offers his own prophecy: he establishes a new future for Israel. He offers the nation a new hope. The two promises of the patriarchal faith-stories had been met. The third had not come from this tribal tradition. J added it to the tradition, by the authority of his own prophetic inspiration (von Rad, p. 23).

J did not want the nation to abandon its future with God. Now that the old promises had been fulfilled, Israel faced the risk of becoming comfortable, of living with the present rather than preparing for the future, of succumbing to despair, rather than risking their security for what was to come. Once again God challenged Israel by offering them a new future with Him. He wanted them, in J's view, to accept risk, to be on the move. He wanted them to trust Him to guide them to a future they could hardly discern. In short, J wanted Israel to remain what it had always been: a nation of hope.

J originated the faith-stories in the Old Testament. The protagonist of each of the faith-stories sums up in his personality those internal attitudes and external actions which were essential for the whole nation of hope. A careful examination of these personal qualities reveal precisely — in what way each protagonist became a model for the hope which the national consciousness expected of each member of Israel.

## The Story of Adam and Eve

The serpent was the most subtle of all the wild beasts that Yahweh God had made. It asked the woman: 'Did God really say you were not to eat from any of the trees in the garden?' The woman answered the serpent: 'We may eat the fruit of the trees in the garden. But of the fruit of the tree in the middle of the garden God said: "You must not eat it, nor touch it, under pain of death." ' Then the serpent said to the woman: 'No! You will not die! God knows in fact that on the day you eat it your eyes will be opened and you will be like gods, knowing good and evil.'

The woman saw that the tree was good to eat and pleasing to the eye, and that it was desirable for the knowledge that it could give. So she took some of its fruit and ate it. She gave some also to her husband who was with her, and he ate it. Then the eyes of both of them were opened and they realized that they were naked. So they sewed fig-leaves together to make themselves loin-cloths.

The man and his wife heard the sound of Yahweh God walking in the garden in the cool of the day, and they hid from Yahweh God among the trees of the garden. But Yahweh God called to the man. 'Where are you?' he asked. 'I heard the sound of you in the garden'; he replied 'I was afraid because I was naked, so I hid.' 'Who told you that you were naked?' he asked 'Have you been eating of the tree I forbade you to eat?' The man replied, 'It was the woman you put with me; she gave me the fruit, and I ate it.' Then Yahweh God asked the woman: 'What is this you have done?' The woman replied: 'The serpent tempted me and I ate.'

Then Yahweh God said to the serpent: 'Because you have done this,
  Be accursed beyond all cattle,
  all wild beasts.
  You shall crawl on your belly and eat dust
  every day of your life.
  I will make you enemies of each other:
  you and the woman,
  your offspring and her offspring.
  It will crush your head
  and you will strike its heel.'
  To the woman he said:
  'I will multiply your pains in childbearing,
  you shall give birth to your children in pain.

Your yearning shall be for your husband,
yet he will lord it over you.'

To the man he said: 'Because you listened to
the voice of your wife and ate from the tree of
which I had forbidden you to eat,

Accursed be the soil because of you.
With suffering shall you get your food from it
every day of your life.
It shall yield you brambles and thistles,
and you shall eat wild plants.
With sweat on your brow
shall you eat your bread,
until you return to the soil,
as you were taken from it.
For dust you are
and to dust you shall return.'

The man named his wife 'Eve' because she was
the mother of all those who live. Yahweh God
made clothes out of skins for the man and his
wife, and they put them on. Then Yahweh God
said: 'See, the man has become like one of us,
with his knowledge of good and evil. He must
not be allowed to stretch his hand out next and
pick from the tree of life also, and eat some and
live for ever.' So Yahweh God expelled him from
the garden of Eden, to till the soil from which he
had been taken. He banished the man, and in
front of the garden of Eden he posted the
cherubs, and the flame of a flashing sword, to
guard the way to the tree of life (Gen. 3:1-24).

The serpent depicts the gods as superior beings
"knowing good and evil." The phrase translates the
Hebrew *yodʻey ṭōv waraʻ*. The Hebrew verb *ydʻ*, "to
know" also has the connotation "to experience."
The phrase *ṭōv waraʻ* is a Hebrew idiom for "everything" (von Rad, p. 86). So the crux of the diabolical invitation is that the serpent holds out the false
hope to man that "You will experience everything!"

Yet this diabolical claim that "You will experience everything!" actually plants the seed for man's despair. For the invitation (an inversion of the divine summons to cooperate with God) opens up to man the possibility that he can extend his own reach beyond the limits set for him by God at creation. The serpent suggests that man can increase his life's power. He not only hints at intellectual enrichment, but suggests that man can be familiar with and triumph over those very mysteries of life which now elude him. For J this is the core of man's fall from God. Precisely here does man separate himself from God again and again throughout history. The fall is not so much a fall into moral evil, into the subhuman. Rather, its essence is man's attempt to escape beyond his human lot. He wants to enjoy a god-like control over his own self and his world. In this Titanic pride man wants to leap out of history and wrench it to his will. And since this contradicts his very nature as a creature bound to history, it remains the source of man's constant sin and of his perennial bout with despair (von Rad, p. 87).

The serpent instills the desire for the whole universe of experience. He urges man to surge ahead of himself instead of waiting upon God. He entices him to act out his victory over the world and gain his complete self before the time predetermined for him by God. He tells man to refuse to acknowledge the limits of human existence. He lures him with the false hope that man can place himself out of time; he pretends that man can obtain his own future before it falls due. He makes man believe he can speed up history and control it, rather than face the fact that he is in history as God's steward. It is the false hope that man can gain the joy of possession before its proper time. It reminds one of the laborer who wants to see the finished product but will not admit the hard work required to create it. Or the student who wants the university degree but refuses to acknowledge the need for diligent study on his part in order to earn it. In short, it is the desire to leap over time rather than live it step by step and minute by minute. To refuse to acknowledge the requirements of the present is to lose one's own future. In the end, the serpent brings man to despair. For hope disappears as soon as one possesses the joy which he sought. The joy falls flat, for, since it is not the fruition of man's cooperation with God, it is not the joy meant for man. As long as man keeps his future in front of him, he can hope. Once he possesses it, he has lost the ability to hope.

The serpent leads man into this despair by three steps. He plays on the whole scale of human emotions, digging deeper and deeper into man's nature, involving his whole being in the act. The fruit is "good to eat," an appeal to man's sense appetite. Second, it is "pleasing to the eye," which attracts his aesthetic sense. Thirdly, it is "desirable for the knowledge it could give," an incitement to man's highest faculty, his mind (von Rad, p. 87). *Nothing the world has to offer — the sensual body, the lustful eye, pride in possessions — could ever come from the Father but only from the world* (I John 2:16). So Eve plucked and ate. Her human pride, the desire to achieve her own future without God, motivated her. And Adam followed suit.

In this way Adam and Eve wanted to tell God how to relate to them rather than to accept His terms. For J, man's perennial error is that he believes he can comprehend God from his own freely predetermined viewpoint, and not, as God would have it, by freely subjecting himself to the divine Word (von Rad, p. 86). He wants to dictate to God the terms of his relationship with mankind. He wants the freedom to determine how God will meet him. He is too proud to admit that God enjoys that very freedom, only much more so, since He is the Creator, beyond the limits imposed on man. He enters history when He wants to. The great lesson of humility for man is to accept this: both the absence and the intervention of God in human history. He comes when He wants to and on His own terms. Man has changed his relationship to God. God does the same: the Creator becomes the Judge. God did not come to man as Judge; man changed his relationship to God and placed himself in this relationship. The lord of creation became the defendant before the divine tribunal.

God comes to man to question him. Why does he hide from God? Has he transgressed the divine commandment? Adam answers: "It was the woman you put with me." Adam tries to place the blame on God for his plight. He wants to exonerate himself. He seeks out the ultimate cause for his own personal disaster, but he cannot admit to God or to himself his own responsibility for the act.

Adam's evasive reply testifies to one of the great traumatic effects of sin. Moreover, it is the source of much of man's despair. Adam has now been joined to his wife in a new bond of unity formed by their sin and disobedience. But neither Adam nor Eve will accept the reality of this communal bond. Man prefers to accept the grim end of community rather than admit to a fellowship created by sin. In God's sight both have achieved a new solidarity, the solidarity of sin. But neither will recognize it or admit it (von Rad, p. 89).

And now God pronounces His judgment on the serpent, the woman and the man. For J, the curses summed up the lot of animals and man which he saw around him: the hostility between snakes and men, the labor pains of women, the harsh task of wresting a living out of the soil.

God's curse on the serpent includes the lines: "It[7] will crush your head / and you will strike its heel" (Gen. 3:15). Apparently J did not consider this text a *protoevangelium*, that is, the first glimmer of salvation history. J does not see primitive history in itself as salvific. Thus, as far as primitive history goes, J does not announce a foreseeable hope for man. He does not acknowledge that man can achieve some type of victory over the force of evil. Rather, he sketches out a real doom for man! He sees man engaged in a hopeless struggle with the serpent. Both will ruin each other in their constant conflict. For J this was an aetiology for the constant hostility which he witnessed between men and snakes, each trying to destroy the other. J does not foresee a final victory of the woman's posterity over the serpent's. Rather, he pictures man and serpent in constant battle with one another (von Rad, p. 90).

The punishment meted out both to the woman and the man strike at the very root of their beings. The woman is to have pain in being a wife and

---

[7]In the MT the masculine pronounce *hû'* refers back to the masculine noun *zar'ă,* "her seed," or "her offspring." MT seems to describe a perennial battle between snakes and mankind. "Offspring" is in this text a collective noun, meaning "mankind" and not one specific individual. LXX translates the pronoun as "he," and refers the text to the coming of the Messiah. This makes the text into the *protoevangelium,* or the first announcement of salvation history, a glimmer of hope amidst the curses which God is imposing on man. The Church fathers followed the LXX reading. The Latin text has "she" and was used in the Western Church to refer to the Virgin Mary who gave birth to the Son who defeated Satan. The present writer is following the J tradition. This is not necessarily the view of the final redactor of the Pentateuch nor the official Church position. See von Rad, p. 90.

mother. The man's punishment also penetrates into the very root of his life: he will suffer as he works to provide sustenance for his family (von Rad, p. 91).

For J the first note of hope in the story on the man's part is his naming of his wife. He connects her name Eve, (in Hebrew *Hawwah*) with the word "to live," (*ḥyh*). It is an act of hope, not hope in promises which lie hidden behind the punishments meted out by God. J does not see this as a supernatural hope aware of the possibility of salvation history. Rather, J portrays an act of hope which embraces human life as such. Man's hope begins with his acceptance that the woman can initiate and continue the great miracle and mystery of bringing forth life by her role as wife and mother. So man begins to assert his own claim against hardship and death.

He opts for life and hope; and he refuses to yield to despair and death. In spite of all the punishment which he and his wife must endure, he comes to terms with his own humanity. Human life must be maintained and not forfeited. The woman passes on the gift of life as well as the heritage of death. Adam takes and blesses this continuance of life, even though he recognizes the grim reality of death (von Rad, p. 93).

He knows he is naked; he knows he has sexual powers. He will not despair because of this. He will employ his sexual powers with his wife to assert his own hope in the value of being human.

God expels Adam and Eve from Paradise. Man has irretrievably lost Eden. He now enters a life of trouble, plagued by the riddle of what he could have been. He begins a life permeated by a remorseless and endless struggle with the powers of evil. In a sense, he fights a losing battle with the power of evil, for he is irremediably subject to the majesty of death (von Rad, p. 98). But he does not despair. He will not destroy himself, but continue himself through his future children.

Even if J did not intend them to do so, Gen. 2 and 3 contain an implied eschatology. In his depiction of primitive history, he treats of the themes of Paradise, the first man, peace among the animals, abundance of water, etc. All of these will reappear in the future development of eschatology (von Rad, p. 99). The past which man had lost became the future which he looked forward to. The story of how despair entered into man's present became the foundation for his hope of a future yet to be.

## The Story of Noah

When Lamech was a hundred and eighty-two years old he became the father of a son. He gave him the name Noah because, he said: 'Here is one who will give us, in the midst of our toil and the laboring of our hands, a consolation derived from the ground that Yahweh cursed' (Gen. 5:28-30).

Yahweh saw that the wickedness of man was great on the earth, and that the thoughts in his heart fashioned nothing but wickedness all day long. Yahweh regretted having made man on the earth, and his heart grieved. 'I will rid the earth's face of man, my own creation,' Yahweh said, 'and of animals also, reptiles too, and the birds of heaven; for I regret having made them.' But Noah had found favor with Yahweh (Gen. 6:5-8).

Yahweh ordered Noah to build an ark, and when it was finished,

Yahweh said to Noah: 'Go aboard the ark, you and all your household, for you alone among this generation do I see as a good man in my judgment. Of all the clean animals you must take seven of each kind, both male and female; of the unclean animals you must take two, a male and its female (and of the birds of heaven also, seven of each kind, both male and female), to propagate their kind over the whole earth. For in seven days' time I mean to make it rain on the earth for forty days and nights, and I will rid the earth of every living thing that I made.' Noah did all that Yahweh ordered (Gen 7:1-5).

And Yahweh closed the door behind Noah.

The flood lasted forty days on the earth . . . Everything with the breath of life in its nostrils died, everything on dry land. Yahweh destroyed every living thing on the face of the earth, man and animals, reptiles, and the birds of heaven. He rid the earth of them, so that only Noah was left, and those with him in the ark (Gen. 7:16-17; 22-23).

Noah, a tiller of the soil, was the first to plant the vine. He drank some of the wine, and while he was drunk he uncovered himself inside his tent (Gen. 9:20-21).

The story of Noah and the flood is a tale of God's eschatological judgment. The narrative deliberately reverses the creation narrative. It will take seven days to prepare for the flood; it took seven days to form the world. The animals and man "with the breath of life" are specially noted. They were also singled out in the creation story. God cursed Adam by sending him to work with the soil which would frustrate his labors. Noah also farms, but with a new result. Adam's new shame forced him to clothe himself; Noah's new-found joy has him return to the primitive nakedness of Eden.

In this J account Lamech predicts the future. After man's long experience with sorrow on earth, he prophesies that his son would bring the first glimmer of worldly hope to men of the future. God's curse on the soil typifies man's estrangement from God. Noah's victory over the soil would be the first glimmer of a new future (von Rad, p. 70).

P explicitly has God tell Noah that He will drown the world soon in His universal judgment upon mankind. But J does not have God tell Noah His future plans. All Noah knows is that God wants him to build an ark. Noah does not learn about the flood until it is time to embark. In this way, J portrays Noah as a man of hope, since Noah must complete the ark (probably on dry land!) without knowing God's intentions. While Noah sweats and labors over his huge ark, while neighbors mock and the years go by, Noah's only consolation is that he is heeding the divine summons. He actively cooperates with God's request to work with Him in the course of world history. Yet he does not know what his own role will be nor the reason for his own arduous activity. Thus Yahweh tested Noah. Noah proved himself to be a man who could work together with God for a future he did not yet see (von Rad, p. 116).

The flood story tells a tale of God's universal eschatological judgment. *Nor did he spare the world in ancient times: it was only Noah he saved, the preacher of righteousness, along with seven others, when he sent the flood over a disobedient world.* (II Pet. 2:5). The story offers a prototype of the Day of the Lord, when His terrifying world judgment will sweep away all opposition to the divine will, just as storm waters surge over all obstacles. Yet this story of cosmic judgment also testifies to God's saving grace. For Noah's frail bark sails precariously above the raging seas. The ark manages to save men and even the animals! J relishes this last item: for the saving of the animals indicates the extent of God's concern for salvation. Even when He plans to sweep the world clean of wicked men, God remembers to keep some of the animals safe! (cf. Jon. 4:11) And God's grace also preserves men, through the man of hope, Noah (von Rad, p. 126).

After disembarking, Noah brings men their great comfort. J considers him the first man to cultivate the grape and process wine. His great discovery offers man a comforting amelioration of his lot. Noah fulfills his father Lamech's prophecy. Adam brought a curse on the soil; Noah is the first man to bring a blessing out of it. Until Noah, man wrestles with the soil to gain a meager livelihood. Now he can have pleasure from the fruit of his labors.

Through Noah God gave man the vine. Human hope begins here; for this is man's first victory over the cosmos which bears God's curse. In the Old Testament, the Israelites considered this plant the noblest of all. For an Israelite, to possess a vineyard, to enjoy its fruit, and to rest in the peace of its cool shade was true bliss and a foretaste of the Messianic Kingdom.[8]

## The Story of Abraham

Yahweh said to Abram 'Leave your country, your family and your father's house, for the land I will show you. I will make you a great nation; I will bless you and make your name so famous that it will be used as a blessing.

I will bless those who bless you:
I will curse those who slight you.
All the tribes of the earth
shall bless themselves by you.'

So Abram went as Yahweh told him, and Lot went with him. Abram was seventy-five years old when he left Haran. Abram took his wife Sarai, his nephew Lot, all the possessions they had amassed and the people they had acquired in

---

[8]von Rad, p. 132, Later, the vineyard would become a symbol for Israel, the nation of hope. Further, Israelites believed wine would be the drink served at the great Messianic banquet at the end of the ages. Jesus himself noted this in many of His parables about the coming kingdom.

Haran. They set off for the land of Canaan, and [eventually] arrived there.

Abram passed through the land as far as Shechem's holy place, the Oak of Moreh. At that time the Canaanites were in the land. Yahweh appeared to Abram and said: 'It is to your descendants that I will give this land.' So Abram built there an altar for Yahweh who had appeared to him. From there he moved on to the mountainous district east of Bethel, where he pitched his tent, with Bethel to the west and Ai to the east. There he built an altar to Yahweh and invoked the name of Yahweh. Then Abram made his way stage by stage to the Negeb (Gen. 12:1-9).

We have now reached the principal figure in J's account. Abraham stands out as the major man of hope in his narrative. He is the link between primitive history and sacred history: the first man to hope in God's salvific will. As we mentioned before, J's account of primitive history pictures an increasing gulf between man and God. J's primitive history ends with God's universal judgment on the sinful nations of men. The account leaves us with the disturbing question: how does God save man? We have already learned how He judges man: with swift and cosmic destruction. Left unanswered, this question can only lead to despair. But J *does* answer the question. His Gen. 12 solves primitive history's unanswered puzzle. He introduces the reader to Abraham and the beginning of sacred history.

When God initiates sacred history, the prototype of all men of faith reacts with a response of hope. The true founder of the nation of hope is a man of hope. But Abraham is more than an example for *Israel.* We have already noted J's prophetic addition to the blessing of Abraham. The ancestor of the nation of hope bears the name by which *all* nations will bless themselves. Abraham's hope has become universal in meaning: all men are to relate to God's saving will by the same act. J reveals the nature of God's saving will. It is universal in scope. It extends beyond the nation of hope to "all the tribes of the earth." J does not consider this a poetic hyperbole, but a sober assessment of the role of Abraham and his descendants. They are the cooperators of salvation history. They bring a supernatural hope to all of mankind (von Rad, pp. 149-150).

In a few short lines J makes Abraham into the man of hope *par excellence.* We moderns can hardly appreciate the totalness of Abraham's trust and confidence in God. He truly hopes in the future which God has offered him. To ask an ancient man to leave his father's household and to break the bond with his ancestors was to demand of him an almost impossible task (von Rad, p. 157). We might compare it with a modern man who apostasized from his religion, renounced his national citizenship, and liquidated his bank account. Then he takes the money, goes to an airline office, hands all the money over to the agent, and says: "Sell me a ticket to any place which this amount will buy." In short, Abraham's act is a decisive option for risk and the complete lack of surety for the future.

Yet without a murmur, Abraham goes, after gathering his family and his goods. Where? He does not know! Like Noah, he works toward a future which he does not see. All he knows is that God will show him his future, and for that he leaves! So he inaugurates the grand march of all the pilgrim people of God who will follow him. The true sons of Abraham are all those who head for a destiny which they have not understood, but which God has summoned them to share with Him. In complete uncertainty, Abraham sets out for a land which "I will show you." His knowledge of his goal comes later! First, he must accept the divine invitation to share his future with God. Without any knowledge of the goal of his journey, he must start moving, for wandering in trust and confidence reveals his own hope in God. He abandons the security of his home; he accepts the life of risk. He leaves Haran a man of hope, his only assets his family, his goods, and his assent to the divine invitation (von Rad, p. 161).

Abraham travels through the land of his inheritance. The Canaanites have complete control over it. Yet he does not question God. He is told that this is to be his inheritance, and he accepts God's word. What an act of hope for a lonely homeless nomad who could see the great cities and armies of the pagans all around him! Yet he trusted in God's word and kept moving. He comes to the "Negeb." The best translation for this Hebrew term would probably be "dryland," and it would mean the same as the English "desert." In his humorous way, J draws a distinct contrast between God's magnificent promises to Abraham and his uneventful trudge through a parched land. God has promised to bring him to a land of plenty and the man of hope finds himself in an arid wasteland! The author hints at problems to come (von Rad, p. 161).

When famine came to the land Abram went down into Egypt to stay there for the time, since the land was hard pressed by the famine. On the threshold of Egypt he said to his wife Sarai: 'Listen! I know you are a beautiful woman. When the Egyptians see you they will say: "That is his wife," and they will kill me but spare you. Tell them you are my sister, so that they may treat me well because of you and spare my life out of regard for you.' When Abram arrived in Egypt the Egyptians did indeed see that the woman was very beautiful. When Pharaoh's officials saw her they sang her praises to the Pharaoh and the woman was taken into Pharaoh's palace. He treated Abraham well because of her, and he received flocks, oxen, donkeys, men and women slaves, she-donkeys and camels. But Yahweh inflicted severe plagues on Pharaoh and his household because of Abram's wife Sarai. So Pharaoh summoned Abram and said: 'What is this you have done to me? Why did you not tell me she was your wife? Why did you say: "She is my sister," so that I took her for my wife? Now, here is your wife. Take her and go!' Pharaoh committed him to men who escorted him back to the frontier with his wife and all he possessed (Gen. 12:10-20).

Soon the arid land besets Abraham with great difficulties. Famine comes to the Holy Land! (von Rad, p. 37) Can Abraham pass this severe test? Sadly, he fails. He sets his course for Egypt; he reverses the route of the Exodus. He plays salvation history backward, depending on the richness of the same land of plenty which would betray his descendants into slavery.

Abraham's callous use of his wife to preserve his own life offends us today. Frequently contemporary commentators attempt to dilute his guilt by emphasizing the slow growth of Israel toward a high moral code. But there is no need to excuse this behavior. For J, this act is a failure on the part of Abraham. He is not censuring him for giving his wife over to Pharaoh's pleasure. Rather J is censuring Abraham for not continuing to trust in Yahweh's care. He should not be in this land of ease at all! J shows what happens when the man of hope relies too much on his own ability and not enough on the grace of God. The mother of the nation winds up in a harem, and the father must be lectured on moral responsibility by the same ruler who would later symbolize evil and oppression!

The story of the preservation of the ancestress occurs again in two parallel passages in Genesis (chapters 20 and 26). The ancients placed great importance on her role. The stories emphasize her beauty, and the importance of preserving her. She was the woman who would bring them forth as a people.

Abraham has refused to trust Yahweh and remain in the land of promise. In despair over the famine, he retreats into Egypt. There is no risk in Egypt, for all his needs are met immediately. Abraham opts for self-preservation; he abandons the risk involved in continuing to hope in the promise made to him by God. In order to save himself, he trusts in his own wit rather than in God's salvific will. Suddenly God's rejection of this view comes upon men. His judgment of wrath falls upon the Egyptians, a preview of the plagues which Moses will inflict on them later. Pharaoh is forced to put Abraham on the Exodus route: he must go back to the land of famine, risk and promise. The man of hope cannot live in the land where all his needs are met, for then he begins to trust in himself and not in God.

Abraham's failure underscores the dilemma which the ancient Israelites suffered. The divine promise brought both confusion and comfort to them. True, they were the heirs of the promise, and a sign of hope to men. But once they made that promise into a guarantee for self-preservation, they trusted more in themselves than in God. The promise brought both salvation and judgment to them. As soon as they abandoned the hope which the promise required, judgment came down from heaven, afflicting both them and other men too.

Yet the lesson remains: Abraham fails, but God remains faithful to His promise. The lesson for the man of hope is meant for the whole nation of hope which descends from him. The crux of the story of

Abraham in Egypt is precisely this: God remains faithful to His salvific will for man, even while the recipients of the promise betray it. Whether punishing him or saving him, God stays with Abraham (von Rad, p. 37). And so it would be with Israel.

Abram's wife Sarai had borne him no child, but she had an Egyptian maidservant named Hagar. So Sarai said to Abram: 'Listen, now! Since Yahweh has kept me from having children, go to my slave-girl. Perhaps I shall get children through her.' Abram agreed to what Sarai had said.

Thus after Abram had lived in the land of Canaan for ten years Sarai took Hagar her Egyptian slave-girl and gave her to Abram as his wife. He went to Hagar and she conceived. And once she knew she had conceived, her mistress counted for nothing in her eyes. Then Sarai said to Abram: 'May this insult to me come home to you! It was I who put my slave-girl into your arms but now she knows that she has conceived, I count for nothing in her eyes. Let Yahweh judge between me and you.' 'Very well,' Abram said to Sarai 'your slave-girl is at your disposal. Treat her as you think fit.' Sarai accordingly treated her so badly that she ran away from her.

The angel of Yahweh met her near a spring in the wilderness, the spring that is on the road to Shur. He said: 'Hagar, slave-girl of Sarai, where have you come from, and where are you going?' 'I am running away from my mistress Sarai,' she replied. The angel of Yahweh said to her: 'Go back to your mistress and submit to her.' The angel of Yahweh said to her: 'I will make your descendants too numerous to be counted.' Then the angel of Yahweh said to her:

'Now you have conceived,
and you will bear a son,

and you shall name him Ishmael,

for Yahweh has heard your cries of distress.

A wild-ass of a man he will be,

against every man, and every man against him,

setting himself to defy all his brothers.'

Hagar bore Abram a son, and Abram gave to the son that Hagar bore the name Ishmael (Gen. 16:1-12; 15).

This narrative introduces the E stream into the Pentateuch tradition. Yahweh does not speak directly to the girl, but through a representative, "His angel." The major part of the story comes from J, however, who presupposes that his readers are familiar with Mesopotamian law. According to that law, a barren wife could offer her slave-girl to her husband. The child would be born "on her knees," and could be adopted as the official and legal heir.

Even after God's glorious promise, Abraham and Sarai remain sterile. Year follows year without the birth of the promised son. Slowly their trust and confidence in God wane. Both lose hope in their future, for the heart of the promise made to them is the birth of a son. How can they bring forth a nation of hope from their marriage, when they have yet to produce a single child? There is no human reason for them to hope any more. There is no heir to carry the promise made to Abraham into the future.

As her hope fades, Sarai loses confidence in Yahweh's control over her own ability to bring forth new life. Rather than trust in Him, she relies on her own wit. She has determined that she can no longer have children, so she induces Abraham to take her maid as wife instead. But by doing this, both she and her husband deny the very foundation on which the promise has been made. Their future belongs to God, and they try to take it over on their own terms. They will no longer wait upon God;

they will base their hopes on their own intelligence. Abraham, the father of the nation of hope, goes to the bed of an Egyptian slave-girl. His descendants would escape from the slavery of Egypt; he joins his seed with it! Once again Abraham is reversing the Exodus experience. Such a reversal cannot typify hope, but only frustration.

Frustration and despair strike Abraham's household as soon as the maid realizes that she has conceived a child. Sarai is unhappy; Hagar is persecuted; and Abraham compromised. No longer living by hope in God, the harmony of the little community disintegrates.

But Yahweh stays with the unfortunate Hagar, promising her that her son would live to father a great people too. But Ishmael, begotten in defiance and lack of faith, cannot be the child of the promise (von Rad, p. 37). He can never be a sign of hope for men, for he had not been born out of hope. He could not father the nation of hope, for he had been conceived when Abraham and Sarai did not trust in God but in themselves. He will father the desert Arabs. The story forms an etiology (from the Israelite point of view) of the constant conflict between the Arabs and Israel. When the ancestor of the nation of hope abandoned his hope in God for a while, then the father of their violent neighbors was born.

Genesis 17 records the P tradition of the covenant made between Abram and Yahweh. His former name was changed to Abraham, and Sarai became Sarah.

Yahweh appeared to Abraham at the Oak of Mamre while he was sitting by the entrance of the tent during the hottest part of the day. He looked up, and there he saw three men standing near him. As soon as he saw them he ran from the entrance of the tent to meet them, and bowed to the ground. 'My lord,' he said, 'I beg you, if I find favor with you, kindly do not pass your servant by. A little water shall be brought; you shall wash your feet and lie down under the tree. Let me fetch a little bread and you shall refresh yourselves before going further. That is why you have come in your servant's direction.' They replied: 'Do as you say.'

Abraham hastened to the tent to find Sarah. 'Hurry,' he said, 'knead three bushels of flour and make loaves.' Then running to the cattle Abraham took a fine and tender calf and gave it to the servant, who hurried to prepare it. Then taking cream, milk and the calf he had prepared, he laid it all before them, and they ate while he remained standing near them under the tree.

'Where is your wife Sarah?' they asked him. 'She is in the tent,' he replied. Then his guest said: 'I shall visit you again next year without fail, and your wife will then have a son.' Sarah was listening at the entrance of the tent behind him. Now Abraham and Sarah were old, well on in years, and Sarah had ceased to have her monthly periods. So Sarah laughed to herself, thinking: 'Now that I am past the age of child-bearing, and my husband is an old man, is pleasure to come my way again!' But Yahweh asked Abraham: 'Why did Sarah laugh and say: "Am I really going to have a child now that I am old?" Is anything too wonderful for Yahweh? At the same time next year I shall visit you again and Sarah will have a son.' 'I did not laugh,' Sarah said, lying because she was afraid. But he replied: 'Oh yes, you did laugh.' (Gen. 18:1-15).

Family harmony, overgenerous hospitality, and docile servants — a community feeling has returned to Abraham's household. A glimpse of hope can be seen. But the delay of the promise has now reached the point at which its fulfillment is apparently impossible (von Rad, p. 214). God visits Abraham to tell him that the message of hope has reached its stage of fulfillment. The promise comes true in a year! Abraham's silence seems to betoken an assent. The man of hope has learned to trust in the unbelievable. But Sarah's laugh of ridicule typifies another attitude. She reveals that man too often regards God's message about his own future as so incredible that it strikes him as ridiculous. *But they laughed at Jesus, knowing she was dead* (Luke 8:53). God has promised Sarah and Abraham grace and salvation. On the other hand, God warns the family of Lot of His coming wrath and judgment upon Sodom. Lot's future sons-in-law react with this laughter of scorn, too (Gen. 19:14). Sarah and they have the same reason for their ridicule. Neither can accept the message that God shares their future with them. When God promises salvation, it appears ridiculous. That is not reason enough to hope. When he warns of His coming judgment, that appears ridiculous too. That is not reason enough to despair (von Rad, p. 214).

Yahweh dealt kindly with Sarah as he had said, and did what he had promised her. So Sarah conceived and bore a son to Abraham in his old age, at the time God had promised. Abraham named the son born to him Isaac, the son to whom Sarah had given birth. Abraham circumcized his son Isaac when he was eight days old, as God had commanded him. Abraham was a hundred years old when his son Isaac was born to him. Then Sarah said: 'God has given me cause to laugh; all those who hear of it will laugh with me.' She added:

'Who would have told Abraham
that Sarah would nurse children!
Yet I have borne him a child in his old age'
(Gen. 21:1-7).

Sarah's laugh of ridicule has been turned by God into a true laugh of joy. She now possesses the promised son, and laughs in possessing her share in the future of the nation of hope. God's message does not seem ridiculous now; she has in her hands the infant who is the pledge of the promise. The couple name him *yishaq*, from the verb *shq*, "to laugh." Isaac = "he laughs." What an appropriate name for the child who brought hope back to the old couple! The proper response to God's invitation to share His future with them is joy. The father, the mother and the child laugh out loud, for this family will banish despair from the world.

I would like to see a theology which is a rediscovery of the celebrative aspects of life, the goodness of the flesh, the wonderful gift of joy, and which at the same time does not become lost in a wallowing in that discovery, but also affirms our hope for the future.[9]

## The Story of Isaac

It happened some time later that God put Abraham to the test. 'Abraham, Abraham,' he called. 'Here I am,' he replied. 'Take your son,' God said, 'your only child Isaac, whom you love, and go to the land of Moriah. There you shall offer him as a burnt offering, on a mountain I will point out to you.'

Rising early next morning Abraham saddled his ass and took with him two of his servants and his son Isaac. He chopped wood for the burnt offering and started on his journey to the place God had pointed out to him. On the third day Abraham looked up and saw the place in the

---

[9]Harvey Cox, "The Problem of Continuity," in *The Future of Hope*. Ed. Frederick Herzog. (New York: Herder and Herder, 1970), p. 80. Hereafter cited as: Herzog.

distance. Then Abraham said to his servants: 'Stay here with the donkey. The boy and I will go over there; we will worship and come back to you.'

Abraham took the wood for the burnt offering, loaded it on Isaac, and carried in his own hands the fire and the knife. Then the two of them set out together. Isaac spoke to his father Abraham: 'Father,' he said. 'Yes, my son,' he replied. 'Look,' he said, 'here are the fire and the wood, but where is the lamb for the burnt offering?' Abraham answered: 'My son, God himself will provide the lamb for the burnt offering.' Then the two of them went on together.

When they arrived at the place God had pointed out to him, Abraham built an altar there, and arranged the wood. Then he bound his son Isaac and put him on the altar on top of the wood. Abraham stretched out his hand and seized the knife to kill his son.

But the angel of Yahweh called to him from heaven. 'Abraham, Abraham,' he said. 'I am here,' he replied. 'Do not raise your hand against the boy,' the angel said. 'Do not harm him, for now I know you fear God. You have not refused me your son, your only son.' Then looking up, Abraham saw a ram caught by its horns in a bush. Abraham took the ram and offered it as a burnt-offering in place of his son (Gen. 22:1-14).

J has spent a long and careful time preparing for the final birth of Isaac. This story strikes the reader as especially difficult if he has been following the J stories which make the birth of Isaac a long climax of the test of Abraham and Sarah's hope in God. But this story actually belongs to the E tradition, and therefore should be treated as separate from the J series. It is important to realize that the story is as much about Isaac as about his father. The boy probably realizes who the "lamb" will be whom God will provide. He, too, must make an act of hope in God's control over his future — even as it leads him to certain death. The lad does not hesitate, but continues walking "together" with his father. As long as God has promised to stay with them they continue to hope. Their trust and confidence remain in God as they head up the mountain for the dread sacrifice.

For Abraham this new command of God must have been totally incomprehensible. Finally Isaac, the heir of the promise, has come into the world. After a long delay, his son has come. Now the boy has grown, shown the first signs of budding manhood. Suddenly, God summons him to sacrifice his only link with the future. For it is only through Isaac that Abraham's seed can expect to gain the promise which God had offered to him. In Genesis 12:1 ff, Abraham had been asked to cut himself off from his whole past. Now God asks him to give up his whole future, too (von Rad, p. 234).

But E has written this story to emphasize Abraham's own growth in hope. By now the patriarch has learned total trust and confidence in God. Without knowing the outcome, yet totally confident that God would find a way to remain true to His promise, Abraham sets out. Somehow, in a way which he does not understand, his future will be restored to him. And this time Abraham does pass the test of his hope in God. God returns his son — and his future — to this remarkable man. The man of hope, like the nation of hope to come, had to be willing to risk losing all, if he was to gain anything.

The man who hopes in God has been granted a personal relationship with him. If he does not have this personal relationship, then the universal ethical law binds him as his only way of remaining in God's graces. If he does enjoy it, then the maintaining of that personal relationship, the continual trust and confidence in God's sharing with him in his future: this is of paramount importance. All other considerations must yield to it — even ethical law.

Why then did Abraham do it? For God's sake, and (in complete identity with this) for his own sake. He did it for God's sake because God required this proof of his faith; for his own sake he did it in order that he might furnish the proof. The unity of these two points of view is perfectly expressed by the word which has always been used to characterize this situation: it is a trial, a temptation. A temptation — but what does that mean? What ordinarily tempts a man is that which would keep him from doing his duty, but in this case the temptation is itself the ethical — which would keep him from doing God's will.

Here is evident the necessity of a new category if one would understand Abraham. Such a relationship to the deity paganism did not know. The tragic hero does not enter into any private relationship with the deity, but for him the ethical is the divine, hence the paradox implied in his situation can be mediated in the universal.

Abraham cannot be mediated, and the same thing can be expressed also by saying that he cannot talk. As soon as I talk I express the universal, and if I do not do so, no one can understand me. Therefore, if Abraham would express himself in terms of the universal, he must say that his situation is a temptation, for he has no higher expression for that universal which stands above the universal which he transgresses.[10]

---

[10]Sören Kierkegaard, "Fear and Trembling, Problem I," *A Kierkegaard Anthology*. Ed. Robert Bretall. (New York: The Modern Library, 1959), p. 133.

But the situation is not a temptation for Abraham. It is a divine summons, an invitation from God to demonstrate that he does not rely on human terms, but that his hope is so strong that he can plan out the sacrifice of his son. Abraham leaps over the confines of the universal ethical code, for he is totally convinced that God is with him. He is not a murderer, but a man of hope. Israel never interpreted this as meaning that the nation could ignore the universal moral code. As a nation, rather, it bound itself to the code more strongly than any other people. But the story is an example, an example of the extent to which the Israelites realized they themselves must put more trust in God than in human wisdom. They had to hope totally and completely in Him as the guide for their future, even when it seemed they had lost their future.

Isaac married Rebekah, who bore him the twins Esau and Jacob. As the older, Esau was entitled to the promise made to the patriarchs. Esau was a hunter, and a prototype of the older hunting population which lived in Israel before the Israelites. Jacob was a shepherd, a prototype of the nomadic Israelite shepherds who would gain possession of the land. The story of Jacob tricking Esau out of his birthright sums up the history of the Israelites who gradually took over the land from their hunting predecessors. The younger brother wins out over the older, just as the younger people defeated the older populace.

## The Story of Jacob

According to J, Jacob had stolen Esau's birthright, the heritage of the promise made to the patriarchs. Now his twin Esau meant to kill him. Following the advice of his mother, Jacob flees from his father's household.

Jacob left Beersheba and set out for Haran. When he had reached a certain place he passed the night there, since the sun had set. Taking one of the stones to be found at that place, he made it his pillow and lay down where he was. He had a dream: a ladder was there, standing on the ground with its top reaching to heaven; and there were angels of God going up it and coming down. And Yahweh was there, standing over him, saying: 'I am Yahweh, the God of Abraham your father, and the God of Isaac. I will give to you and your descendants the land on which you are lying. Your descendants shall be like the specks of dust on the ground; you shall spread to the west and the east, to the north and the south, and all the tribes of the earth shall bless themselves by you and your descendants. Be sure that I am with you; I will keep you safe wherever you go, and bring you back to this land, for I will not desert you before I have done all that I have promised you' (Gen. 28:10-15).

When Jacob flees from Isaac's household, he finds himself homeless, landless, and penniless. Cursed instead of blessed, he falls asleep exhausted as night comes on. With no roof over his head and a rock for a pillow, he appears cut off from his past and a man with no future before him. Jacob is in a hopeless situation — and just then God comes to him with the promise of hope (von Rad, p. 38). God takes what the thief has done and solemnly ratifies it!

God promises Jacob both land and posterity. The ancient faith of the pre-Mosaic Israelites was grounded on this hope: that God had promised them a share in the tillable land and posterity. This hope, now fulfilled for J's contemporaries, prefigures a new destiny for Jacob (and the nation Israel). For Jacob has now become a sign of salvific hope for all the tribes of the earth. The angels of God travel between heaven and earth on Jacob's ladder. They bring the affairs of men to God and the will of God to men. Jacob — and Israel — were destined to be mediators between God and men.

In vv. 13 and 14 God gives Jacob the general blessing which had been made to all the patriarchs. But in vs. 15 He refers specifically to the special problems now facing Jacob, the landless emigrant. He promises him to ward off the dangers which threaten him; He guarantees him His protection when he leaves the Holy Land, and that He will be with him on his return (von Rad, p. 280).

Jacob goes to Laban's household. Over the years he gains Laban's two daughters in marriage; his sons are born; and he gains possession over many flocks. Rich with wives, children, and animals beyond his wildest dreams, Jacob sets out to return to the Holy Land. For a while he is pursued by Laban, who is angered at his sudden departure and the absence of the household gods. But Jacob manages to placate his father-in-law. Now that he has every reason to trust in his own powers, God does not come with a blessing. Rather, J has him fall upon Jacob in the night like a powerful wrestler (Gen. 32:26). The two stories emphasize that God is inscrutable and perfectly free in how he relates to man. When man has every reason to despair, God offers him hope. When man believes he can control his own future, God comes in the night like a mighty wrestler to knock the presumption out of him.

The J narrative showed Jacob as a mediator between God and man. The P account does not have Jacob trick Esau out of his birthright. Instead of fleeing from the wrath of Esau, P has Isaac commission Jacob to leave and look for a proper wife (Gen. 27:46-28:5). Sending Jacob on his way, Isaac blesses him with the following prayer: *"May El Shaddai bless you; may he make you fruitful and make you multiply so that you become a group of nations "* (Gen. 28:3). This P prayer enhances the J tradition of Jacob (Israel) as a universal mediator between God and men.

For Jacob is to grow into a "group of nations," in Hebrew $q^ehal$ `ammīn`. This term occurs here for the first time in the Old Testament. It refers back to the promise made to Abraham in the P narrative that he would father a "multitude of nations," ($h^amōn$ $gōyim$) in 17:4. This P blessing in 28:3 may imply the universal eschatological cultic community of nations, all bound together by their common worship of the one God. $Q^ehal$ normally refers to the assembly of the community at worship. (von Rad, p. 277). According to P, the nation of hope was destined to inaugurate the final community of mankind into a group of brothers all worshiping the same God.

## The Story of Joseph

Jacob's favorite son, Joseph, frequently told his brothers of special dreams which he had. These presaged a great future for the younger brother. The other sons of Jacob, angered over Joseph's confidence in his own great future, sold the boy into slavery. Slavery took his future away from him.

> If his future is to be created by the masters, he will remain 'object,' and the new future will not be the embodiment of his negation and hope but rather another triumph of the master over him (Alves, p. 14).

No longer the subject of his own destiny, Joseph has lost every human right to hope. Too, Joseph reverses the Exodus experience of his descendants. Unlike Abraham, he does not do this by free choice. Rather, he is forced to leave the freedom of Israel for the slavery of Egypt. He is driven from the land of hope and suffers the end of his own personal freedom. Yet Joseph maintains his personal trust and confidence in God. And that alone justifies his standing as a man of hope. But God will not abandon such a man! Joseph is sold to an Egyptian master. For a while he prospers, then the man's wife falsely accuses Joseph of attacking her. The man sends Joseph off to prison. There he interprets the dreams of Pharaoh's cupbearer and the chief baker. Pharaoh will restore the cupbearer but behead the baker. Joseph asks the cupbearer to remember him when he is restored to freedom. But the man does not, and Joseph remains in prison. God remembers his servant. Through a strange dream He visits Pharaoh, and now the king of Egypt desperately needs someone to interpret the dream for him. God has told Pharaoh something about his future, but without a mediator he has no idea what that future is.

In the morning Pharaoh, feeling disturbed, had all the magicians and wise men of Egypt summoned to him. Pharaoh told them his dream, but no one could interpret it for Pharaoh. Then the chief cupbearer addressed Pharaoh: 'Today I must recall my offenses. Pharaoh was angry with his servants and put myself and the chief baker under arrest in the house of the commander of the guard. We had a dream on the same night, he and I, and each man's dream had a meaning for himself. There was a young Hebrew with us, one of the slaves belonging to the commander of the guard. We told our dreams to him and he interpreted them, giving each of us the interpretation of his dream. It turned out just as he interpreted for us: I was restored to my place, but the other man was hanged.'

Then Pharaoh had Joseph summoned, and they hurried him from prison. He shaved and changed his clothes, and came into Pharaoh's presence. Pharaoh said to Joseph: 'I have had a dream which no one can interpret. But I have heard it said of you that when you hear a dream you can interpret it.' Joseph answered Pharaoh: 'I do not count. It is God who will give Pharaoh a favorable answer.'

So Pharaoh told Joseph: 'In my dream I was standing on the bank of the Nile. And there were seven cows, fat and sleek, coming up out of the Nile, and they began to feed among the rushes. And seven other cows came up after them, starved, ugly and lean; I have never seen such poor cows in all the land of Egypt. The lean and ugly cows ate up the seven fat cows. But when they had eaten them up, it was impossible to tell they had eaten them, for they remained as lean as before. Then I woke up. And then again in my dream, there, growing on one stalk, were seven ears of corn, beautifully ripe; but sprouting up after them came seven ears of corn, withered, meager and scorched by the east wind. The shrivelled ears of corn swallowed the seven ripe ears of corn. I told the magicians this, but no one could tell me the meaning.'

Joseph told Pharoah: 'Pharaoh's dreams are one and the same: God has revealed to Pharaoh what he is going to do. The seven fine cows are seven years and the seven ripe ears of corn are seven years; it is one and the same dream. The seven gaunt and lean cows coming up after them are seven years, as are the seven shrivelled ears of corn scorched by the east wind: there will be seven years of famine. It is as I have told Pharaoh: God has revealed to Pharaoh what he is going to do. Seven years are coming, bringing great plenty to the whole land of Egypt, but seven years of famine will follow them, when all the plenty in the land of Egypt will be forgotten, and famine will exhaust the land. The famine that is to follow will be so very severe that no one will remember what plenty the country enjoyed. The reason why the dream came to Pharaoh twice is because the event is already determined by God, and God is impatient to bring it about.

'Pharaoh should now choose a man who is intelligent and wise to govern the land of Egypt. Pharaoh should take action and appoint supervisors over the land, and impose a tax of one-fifth on the land of Egypt during the seven years of plenty. They will collect all food produced during these good years that are coming. They will store the corn in Pharaoh's name, and place the food in the towns and hold it there. This food will serve as a reserve for the land during the seven years of famine that will afflict the land of Egypt. And so the land will not be destroyed by the famine' (Gen. 41:8-36).

For the most part, this narrative comes from the E tradition. We note immediately a strong emphasis on secular values and human wisdom in the story. Abraham had used his wit to avoid his future with Yahweh when he was in Egypt. But Joseph uses his wisdom in cooperation with God's plan for his future. If J's theology had been misunderstood, it could be thought to advocate a quietism which put God in total command of man's future. But, of course, J did not mean that: he emphasized the need for the man to let God have his role in the working out of the future. This E narrative, however, does present an excellent corrective to any misunderstanding of the J tradition. E strongly underlines the value of man's activity within the world. As long as man recognizes God's preeminence in the working out of his future, true hope demands a personal responsibility for the world to come.

The Pharaoh approaches the problem completely

incorrectly. He presumes that men can gain a knowledge and control over the future by human art. He puts his trust in specially trained seers. In the ancient world Egypt was known for its numerous magicians and sages. But as in the time of Moses, they are totally helpless when faced with a message from the true God. As soon as Joseph hears this misconception, he admonishes the Pharaoh diplomatically about the pathetic error. Pharaoh has treated him as simply another skilled dream specialist. To be sure, he believes him quite superior to the others in the court who are stumped. He does not think Joseph will have to exert himself too much. But Joseph definitively rejects this interpretation of his own role. He cries *"bil 'adāy,"* (Gen. 41:16) the Hebrew term which literally means: "Not in me!" = "It is not my ability at all!" Joseph makes an important theological point. Yes, he does enjoy a charismatic illumination of the future, but it comes only from God (von Rad, p. 370). Further, unlike the practitioners of magic in Egypt, he does not claim any ability to control the future. God has predetermined it; man remains the steward of history and not its master.

Yet Joseph can offer hope to Egypt, because God *does* illumine him. He does not give him a god-like control over the future, but he does grace him with the wisdom to act wisely once the direction of the future is known.

In Joseph's speech to Pharaoh, two things stand out clearly: 1) There is a definite future predetermined by God. God will give it fabric out of His own freedom. Nothing man can do will avert that future. Man remains a creature bound to time; if the future holds famine, he will go through a time of famine. 2) Yet there is no need for men to starve while this future takes place. He can prepare for the future by the appropriate secular measures. Joseph does not order Egyptians into prayer meetings. Since God has decided what their future will be, Joseph tells the community to prepare to meet it with the resources at their disposal. And Pharaoh immediately picks Egypt's best resource, the wise man Joseph, to implement the program outlined by the Hebrew slave. The intelligent man of hope does not just let the future happen to him. No matter how painful the inevitable is, he strengthens himself and his community to meet it properly (von Rad, p. 371).

The famine eventually comes to the Holy Land. Jacob's sons are forced to go to Egypt to buy food from Joseph, but they do not know that the ruler who is supervising the distribution of food is really their brother. After two trips, Joseph finally reveals his true identity to the sons of Jacob: *"I am your brother Joseph whom you sold into Egypt. But now, do not grieve, do not reproach yourselves for having sold me here, since God sent me before you to preserve your lives"* (Gen. 45:4-5).

Joseph's brothers had tried to take his future away from him. But to be a slave *and* have God with him, meant that Joseph could not lose his future. The very means which the brothers employed to frustrate the design of God became the source of Joseph's eventual triumph. The man of hope stays with God and cannot lose his future. The brothers of Joseph sent him into the slavery of Egypt, the very punishment which would befall all of their descendants. Yet this crass deed becomes the very means by which God can "preserve your lives." For the sons of Jacob, the heirs of the promise, would surely have perished in the world-wide famine, if Joseph had not been the steward of all the grain of Egypt. The man of hope used his native wit to prepare the land for its future; he set aside food for the starving. Through his wisdom, God preserved the family which was heir to the promise (von Rad, p. 393). Even when men sin, turn from God's grace, and deny the possibility of the future which He offers them, He stays with the man of hope. Eventually this mediator becomes the means by which God can save the whole people. The rejected mediator returns to those who thrust him aside; he returns with grace and salvation from God. Never does the God of hope abandon His people!

## The Story of Moses

After several generations, the Pharaoh of Egypt forgot the contributions which the Israelite Joseph had made to his country. He oppressed the people of Israel severely. Their bodily needs were well taken care of, for the Israelites remembered *"when we were able to sit down to pans of meat and could eat bread to our heart's content"* (Ex. 16:3). But the nation had no personal freedom; it was not a sign of hope, and God could not permit this. They must have their future restored to them. In their heart of hearts, they were really crying out to be free. And this was the call God heard: not the sighs of satisfaction, but the despair in the heart of those who have no future, no control over their own lives, no freedom to become a people.

The Book of Exodus thus narrates the story of God's decision to liberate His people from the slavery of Egypt. He selects Moses to lead them out of Egypt and into the land of their fathers, Canaan.

Moses looked; there was the bush blazing but it was not being burnt up. 'I must go and look at this strange sight,' Moses said, 'and see why the bush is not burnt.' Now Yahweh saw him go forward to look, and God called to him from the middle of the bush. 'Moses, Moses!' he said. 'Here I am,' he answered. 'Come no nearer,' he said. 'Take off your shoes, for the place on which you stand is holy ground. I am the God of your father,' he said, 'the God of Abraham, the God of Isaac and the God of Jacob.' At this Moses covered his face, afraid to look at God.

And Yahweh said: 'I have seen the miserable state of my people in Egypt. I have heard their appeal to be free of their slave-drivers. Yes, I am well aware of their sufferings. I mean to deliver them out of the hands of the Egyptians and bring them up out of that land to a land rich and broad, a land where milk and honey flow, the home of the Canaanites, the Hittites, the Amorites, the Perizzites, the Hivites and the Jebusites. And now the cry of the sons of Israel has come to me, and I have witnessed the way in which the Egyptians oppress them, so come, I send you to Pharaoh to bring the sons of Israel, my people, out of Egypt.'

Moses said to God: 'Who am I to go to Pharaoh and bring the sons of Israel out of Egypt?' 'I shall be with you,' was the answer (Ex. 3:2-12).

What an unlikely choice for a national liberator! Moses had been raised as an Egyptian so the Israelites would not favor him. He had killed an Egyptian, so the Egyptians would not heed him. He had chosen to live as a voluntary exile far away from the whole business. What drove this desert nomad back into Egypt, to the very scene of his crime, to plead before Pharaoh? Nothing less than a divine commission. God wanted His people to be free, and Moses to be the charismatic leader of that liberation. And what could Moses rely on to sustain him in this great venture? Only that God "will be with him." Just as He sustained the patriarchs, He promises to sustain Moses.

But what of Moses? Only a man of hope could ever heed such a summons. Moses himself had to hope completely in God's power over the future. He had to put his trust and confidence totally in God. For he had no military experience; he had never governed large groups of people. Now he had to take a whole nation and liberate it. The route of salvation begins with one man believing more in God than in himself. There is no human reason why Israel should defeat Egypt. But that is the whole point: the nation of hope is born out of trust in God and not in its own human powers. God gives it the reason for hoping and for being free.

The Book of Exodus tells of the journey from Egypt, through the Reed Sea, and into the Sinai peninsula. It ends with the nation at the foot of Mount Sinai. Exodus is the second book of the Pentateuch. It is a religious epic, that is, a narrative of the origins of a nation's historical, legal, and cultic traditions. The book includes a conglomerate of historical facts, legends, miracle accounts of divine intervention, popular etymologies, written and oral sources, and legal and cultic codes; in short, all those elements which added up to a national consciousness for Israel. As with the rest of the Pentateuch, the key elements in Israel's national consciousness consisted in the persistent themes of promise, election, covenant, and law. God is faithful to His promises. He freely elects the nation Israel as His people and sets aside certain individuals from among them as His charismatic spokesmen. On His own initiative He establishes a lasting covenant with them. He gives them the law as a sign of this mutual commitment. Their obedience to this law signifies that He is their God and they are His people.

At Mount Sinai God gives Israel the legal and cultic code by which they will be known as His people. We must remember that this account represents an archetype for the subsequent religious thought of the whole nation. Thus the story would readily incorporate many incidents of miraculous intervention. Yet the overall sweep does fit into the pattern of secular history.

The Pharaoh who had oppressed the Israelites and whose death suggested the possibility of a revolt was probably Seti I. His oppression continued under Rameses II. Shortly after his accession, the Exodus of Israel out of Egypt took place. Exodus narrates the selection of Moses as the charismatic leader for the Hebrews. According to the faith-story in Exodus, he negotiates with the Pharaoh, who obstinately refuses to let the Israelites leave Egypt. God afflicts the people with 10 plagues, and Pharaoh yields. Finally, Moses can lead the Israelites out of Egypt. On the way they meet many obstacles which God overcomes for them by His miracles.

Exodus is a conflation of J, E, and P. Occasionally D appears also. The final redaction, which we possess today, is dated from the fifth century B.C.[11]

We modern readers must therefore understand that the final form of Exodus was composed eight centuries after the events which it narrates. Therefore, the text obviously contains much of the subsequent theological and historical reflection of the Israelites. They would, of course, explain later liturgical and legal practices which developed after the initial conquest of Canaan by placing them back in the time of Moses. For instance, many of the laws in Exodus presuppose an agricultural economy and the cult of Yahweh at a single place of worship (Jerusalem). Neither of these was known to the original nomads whom Moses led into Sinai.

From the time of Moses the people of Israel began to appear before the world as a nation in their own right. Many of their religious and legal traditions were rooted in his charismatic leadership.

[11]John E. Huesman, S.J. "Exodus." *JBC* I, p. 47.

To E, Moses was the one who began the worship of God under His personal name "Yahweh." According to J, the worship of Yahweh went back to the days before the flood (Gen. 4:26). According to P, Yahweh revealed himself to the patriarchs as "El-Shaddai" (Gen. 17:1ff). We are going to concentrate on the E tradition, because it tells a great deal about the Israelites' consciousness of God as the source of natural hope.

A careful study of the Hebrew text will facilitate this analysis:

> *Wayyo'mer mōšēh 'el-ha'elohīym hinnēh 'ankīy va' 'el-beney yiśra'el we'amartīy lahem 'elohēy 'avōṭēykem šelahnīy 'alēykem we'ameru-līy māh-ššemō māh 'omar 'alēhem* (Ex. 3:13).

> *Wayyo'mer 'elohīym 'el-mošēh 'ehyēh 'aser 'ehyēh* (3:14a) *wayyo'mer kōh to'mar livnēy yiśra'el 'ehyēh šelahnīy 'alēykem* (3:14b).

> *Wayyo'mer 'ōd 'elohīym 'el-mosēh koh-to'mar 'el beney yiśra'el YHWH 'elohēy 'avoṭēykem 'elohēy 'avraham 'elohēy yiṣhaq wē'lohēy ya'aqov šelahnīy 'alēykem zēh-ššemīy le'olam wezēh zikrīy ledor dor* (3:15).

I translate this in the following manner:

And Moses said to God: 'Look! I am to go to the sons of Israel and I am to say to them: "the God of your fathers has sent me to you." And they will say to me: "What is his name?" What am I to say to them?'

And God said to Moses: '*I will be who I will be.*' And he added: 'So you are to speak to the sons of Israel: "*I will be* has sent me to you." '

And again God said to Moses: 'So you are to speak to the sons of Israel: "YAHWEH, the God of your fathers, the God of Abraham, the God of Isaac, and the God of Jacob has sent me to you." This is my name forever and this is my memorial from generation to generation' (Ex. 3:13-15).

The verb forms for God's self-designation are in the Hebrew imperfect, which can usually be translated either as present or future. I have selected the future tense for two reasons: 1) excluding *'ehyēh* six of the thirteen verb forms in this section have a future meaning. The past forms are used for the verbs "to say" and "to send." The "said" forms are obviously the narrative use of the past tense, while the "sent" forms clearly refer to the present divine commission to Moses, which will not be a past event until he does proclaim Israel's liberation to God's people. 2) *'ehyēh* itself has been used in vs. 12 in the future tense: "I will be with you."

This section has had a complex development before reaching its final stage. It is difficult to restore the original E version which began the tradition. S.R. Driver places the entire section within the E tradition and credits J with 3:16-18.[12] On the other hand, A.H. McNeile assigns 3:9-14 to E, 15 to a D editor, and 16-18 to J.[13] The redactor would then have stitched together the E and J versions by using the rare "Yahweh God" of vs. 15. However, if we do omit 15 from the original version, we miss the climax of the revelation of the name "Yahweh." We must admit that the *'ōd* (again) in vs. 15 and the repetition of vs. 15's list of the patriarchs in vs. 16 both suggest a redactor's addition. Whatever final conclusion language scholars draw, I believe we must at least retain the name "Yahweh" in vs. 15 as part of the original E version.

Apparently, in the original E, which has been covered over with more sophisticated theological wording, there was some hesitancy on God's part in

---

[12]*The Book of Exodus* (Cambridge: University Press, 1918) p. xix. Hereafter cited as: Driver.

[13]*The Book of Exodus* (London: Methuen, 1931[iii]), p. xv. Hereafter cited as: McNeile.

the dialogue before Moses learned the name of Yahweh in vs. 15. Is it possible that we once had a long debate in the original E, and all we have now is the question of 13 and the answer of 15? Then 14ab would be an editor's explanatory link. Or can 14a and b be part of the original E debate? Could it be that the original readers of E could readily see the link between the name Yahweh and the verb *'ehyēh* and that a later redactor added 15 to spell out the obvious? We cannot avoid the impression that this section was carefully reworked by a later editor. Nor can we avoid the fact that the answers of 14a and b *do* have an etymological relationship with the Yahweh of vs. 15.

In short, the problem for Biblical scholars is: Is vs. 14 an insertion for the purpose of popular etymology (i.e. Yahweh comes from the verb *hyh* "to be,") or is vs. 15 an addition by an editor who wished to link up this cryptic answer with the traditional Hebrew name for God? Or further, could it be that the whole section is a genuine E tradition which has been radically reedited to correspond with subsequent theological reflection?

M. Noth explored the first two alternatives:

> We cannot of course completely escape the impression that there is some overcrowding in vs. 14f. The threefold introduction to God's speech does not look original; this unusual repetition is stressed rather than explained by the little word [again] at the beginning of vs. 15. If then we must have both primary and secondary materials in these verses, we must hold the simpler expression to be the original and thus should not understand vs. 15 to be a secondary expansion of vs. 14 in the sense of being an explicit interpretation of the *'ehyēh ('ašher 'ehyēh)* through the name Yahweh, especially as vs. 14 could hardly have been in need of such an expressed interpretation.

Instead we should regard the simple giving of the name in vs. 15 as an original answer to the question at the end of vs. 13, in the same way as the sentence in vs. 15b 'This is my name forever,' will then take up the question 'What is his name?' in vs. 13. Verse 14a would then have been added subsequently as an explanation of the name Yahweh and would have been inserted into the context because of 14b which verbally anticipates the following clause. In this way the insertion of the little word ["again"] at the beginning of vs. 15 would eventually commend itself. Should vs. 14a (b) then be a secondary literary element in the material of the E narrative the addition could still be quite old and go back to a perhaps older tradition of the explanation of the name Yahweh.[14]

E most frequently treats God reverently. Perhaps he has deleted an original J version of a market-haggle between Yahweh and Moses. Perhaps even he himself had a market-dialogue version which subsequent editors toned down. I would like to assign the entire section to E. E material does contain popular etymologies, so the answer *Yahweh* in vs. 15 would not be presupposed but actually given in the text. I think each of the statements assigned to God are the original E's. It is Moses' retorts which have probably been excised because of a desire to edify. Moses is engaged in a verbal struggle with God to wrest the divine name from Him. It is similar to the struggle which Jacob once had, according to J. He won a blessing, but not the revelation of the divine name (Gen. 32:23-29). The editor of Exodus removed all of Moses' blatant importunities from the E text.

Therefore, the original version was a popular

---

14*Exodus: A Commentary* (Philadelphia: Westminster, 1962), pp. 43-44. Hereafter cited as: Noth.

etymology by which E tried to explain the origin of the divine name Yahweh. In E this name is first revealed to Moses, and used by him as a guarantee of his divine commission. Exodus has already had two popular E etymologies before this in the text (Ex. 2:10 and 2:22). Unlike these two former ones, this account is in a narrative form, rather than simply tacked on as an explanatory addition.

We must remember that Hebrew etymology in the Bible was not a linguistic science. Rather, it reflected a deep concern about personal names and a concommitant desire to "explain" them. So we have to distinguish between linguistic etymology and popular etymology in the Biblical text. "Most etymologies in the Bible are popular and scientifically incorrect," warns Father John McKenzie.[15] Verbal word-play (paronomasia, or more popularly, punning) abounds in the Biblical explanations of personal names.

In Hebrew speech there is a peculiar association of the person and the name that is foreign to our idiom. 'Name' is used in contexts where modern language uses 'person' or 'self.' To have no name is to have no existence in reality; when one's name is blotted out, one ceases to exist. To give a name is to confer identity and not merely to distinguish from other individuals or species; when God creates (Gen. 1), He gives a name to each object of His creation. The conferring of a name is an act of power and an assertion of ownership or some other form of control. A change of name indicates a change of state or condition, the beginning of a new existence.

To know the name is to know the reality named. For this reason the Old Testament re-

---

**15**"Some Aspects of Old Testament Thought." *JBC* II, p. 738, no. 12. Hereafter cited as: McKenzie.

flects the love of etymologies which, if analyzed linguistically, are fanciful. The name is pregnant with meaning; a connection by paronomasia with the characteristic of a person or an event in his life reveals the person more fully (McKenzie, p. 737).

So we can understand the importance of learning the true name of God.

E's fanciful etymologies can be seen in Ex. 2:22 and 2:10. Moses names his son *Gēršom*, which E explains as coming from the verb *gūr* "to wander." The name is supposedly given because the son was born while Moses was a wanderer in exile, but the derivation is doubtful. More to the point, E tells us in 2:10 that *Mošēh*, the Hebrew for "Moses," comes from the verb *mšh*, "to draw out." Pharaoh's daughter "drew" Moses "out" of the river to save him. Thus he received his name. But linguistically, the name probably comes from the Egyptian *mes*, *mesu*, "child," or "son." Frequently this was part of Egyptian names. But E's explanation not only fits the tradition of Moses' being rescued from infant drowning in the Nile, the name itself also defines his role as national liberator. For Moses was the one who "drew" Israel "out" of Egypt, and "out" of the waters of the Reed Sea. The name might not come from the verb *mšh*, but it does identify Moses and his unique role in the history of the nation of hope. This gives it its validity.

In this section E explains that YHWH comes from *hyh*, "to be." E sees the name as the third person masculine singular of *hyh* = "he will be." Later on, we will explore this meaning more fully. Actually, linguists trace the form YHWH back to *hwh*, a cognate of *hyh*, used in archaic times and in the Arabic contemporary with E. It means "to fall," "to become," and, at times, in Hebrew, "to be."

The name Yahweh was unknown to Hebrew

scholars for centuries. This prevented any serious linguistic studies being made of the form. The text had been misunderstood for centuries. Apparently, the original admonition of Ex. 20:7 not to use the name "Yahweh" meant to be wary of calling upon the personal name of God unless one meant the truth of what he said. In the course of theological development, however, the command gradually took on the literal meaning that no one was to pronounce the name at all. Thus whenever *YHWH* appeared in the older texts the reader would pronounce *'dny*, "Lord," instead. When vowel pointing was added to the texts later on, the consonants *YHWH* were retained, but the vowels for *'adonāy* were written instead. The reader saw *yeh-wah*, but said *adonai*.

> The pronunciation Jehovah is an impossible hybrid, first used, so far as is known, by Peter Galatinus in 1518 A.D. (McNeile, p. 23).

This wrong pronunciation persisted for centuries and prevented any serious linguistic analysis of the word.

Contemporary scholarship has unearthed the original pronunciation. At least, the best conjecture is *yahwēh*, rendered in English by "Yahweh."[16]

The verb form "Yahweh" can be either causative (Hebrew: hiphil) or simple (Hebrew: qal). If we accept the form as a hiphil, the word *hwh* could have the following meanings: "to fall," "to become," or "to be." So Yahweh could mean:

"He Causes to Fall (Rain)" = God, the Rainmaker. In a primitive anthropomorphism, Yahweh would be the god who pulled back the latches of the vault of heaven. This would let "the waters above the heavens" (Gen. 1:7) fall down and water the

---

[16]McNeile, p. 23. The author gives a summary of the ancient authorities who attest to this pronunciation.

earth below. This primitive meaning of the name is supported by the popularity of the worship of the earth god Baal among the early Israelites. If the popular imagination thought that the officially sanctioned God could control only the rainfall, then there would be an obvious temptation to worship the earth god to appease him also and make the crops grow. The official orthodox representatives of the religion would insist that this was a misconception and that Yahweh also controlled the earth processes. This polemical thrust can be seen in the P account of creation (Gen. 1:11-12).

"He Causes to Become" = God, the Former, the Maker — a more developed concept in which Yahweh brought order and form into a chaotic universe. Again, this can be supported by Gen. 1 in the Hebrew text, where certain elements exist already in the universe. Yahweh does not make the world out of nothing, but forms the chaos into something usable and beneficial for man.

"He Causes to Be" = the Creator. This highly sophisticated theological concept makes Yahweh into a God totally independent of the universe. He brings all into existence by himself. In its fullest sense, the causative form of the verb means "He Causes to Be What Comes into Existence."[17] Or "He who causes to come to pass," which means "create, procreate, form, make."[18] This, of course, agrees with the Christian understanding of God as the fullness of being. It falls in line with LXX translation of 14a *egō eimi ho ōn* = "I am the Being."

---

[17]William Foxwell Albright *From Stone Age to Christianity.* (Baltimore: Johns Hopkins, 1940), p. 198.

[18]Frank Moore Cross, Jr. "Yahweh and the God of the Patriarchs," *Harvard Theological Review* LV (1962), p. 253, n. 123.

All of this has certain arguments in its favor, but the difficulty with this interpretation is that it imposes on the verb *hwh* and its cognate *hyh* a metaphysical import. This metaphysical import of static being, which the Greek *einai* can bear, is not really possessed by either Hebrew verb. Neither form implies a self-contained existence. The Hebrew verb "to be" means "to-be-in-relation-to-another." (Recall the "I will be with you" of vs. 12.) It implies that I will "be for you," that is, I will be actively doing something for your benefit.

> We may just observe that the name Yahweh is in fact probably to be derived from the stem *hwh*, frequent in the Aramaic and Arabic dialects, which corresponds to the Hebrew root *hyh*, 'be.' (Noth, p. 44).

> The verb *hyh* in Hebrew does not express pure 'being,' pure 'existing,' but an 'active being' which does not take place just anywhere, but makes its appearance in the world of men and primarily in the history of Israel. This perhaps is what is expressed in Ex. 3:14a to explain the name Yahweh (Noth, p. 45).

Thus it would be better to avoid the hiphil translation and its attendant metaphysics. The form is best translated as a qal. This would seem to correspond closest to E's own understanding of the form: God reveals himself to Moses as the God of the future, who will establish a personal relationship with him and his people Israel. The nation of hope worships the God who promises to be with them and for them as they move forward in their own history to a mutual future with Him.

> In the first place the verb *hāyāh* expresses not to be *essentially*, but to be *phenomenally*; it corresponds to *gignomai* not *einai*; it denotes, in Delitzsch's words, not the idea of inactive, abstract existence, but the active manifestation

of existence. Secondly, the imperfect tense used expressed not a fixed, present state ('I am'), but *action*, either reiterated (habitual) or *future*, i.e., either *I am wont to be* or *I will be* (Driver, p. 40).

The giving of the name follows in vv. 14f., first and foremost through the mysterious sentence '*ehyēh* '*ašer* '*ehyēh*, ... from which the catchword '*ehyēh* ... is taken as the name of the God who appeared to Moses (v. 14). This name unmistakenly hints at the divine name Yahweh insofar as an Israelite ear could immediately understand the transition from '*ehyēh* to *yahwēh* merely as a transition from the first to the third person (in which the *w* of *yahwēh* in place of the *y* of '*ehyēh* may have been felt as dissimilation after the initial *y*) so that the name Yahweh would be understood to mean "he is" (Noth, p. 43).[19]

But the early Hebrew mind was essentially practical, not metaphysical. A. B. Davidson says that the verb 'does not mean "to be" essentially or ontologically, but phenomenally.' He explains it as follows: 'It seems evident that in the view of the writer '*ehyēh* and *yahwēh* are the same: that God is '*ehyēh*, "I will be," when speaking of himself, and *yahwēh*, "he will be," when spoken of by others. What he will be is left unexpressed — he will be with them, "helper, strengthener, deliverer"; the word is explained by the "I will be with thee" of vs. 12' (McNeile, p. 22).

This E narrative has traces which remind the reader of the traditional "market-haggle" motif. In this polemical dialogue, the relationship between the petitioner and God resembles a haggle in the

---

[19]The author disagrees with the present tense "he is."

marketplace between buyer and seller over a price. Our own literary culture enjoys a tradition of a fixed, uniform price on the market.

> The extreme abstraction and detachment represented by our pricing system is quite unthinkable and unusable amidst populations for whom the exciting drama of price haggling occurs with every transaction.[20]

> In an oral culture, such as E lived in polemic becomes a major constituent of actuality, an accepted element of existence of a magnitude no longer appealing to modern technological man (Ong, p. 200).

Therefore, we find it difficult to appreciate the Near Easterner's love for oral combat. To argue and fight for one's own price is considered perfectly natural. A Near Easterner would be surprised if someone paid the first price which he asked.

This view affects the way in which he understands his own relationship with God. God has to be won over, debated with, and finally a victory is scored. Later theological reflection made the Israelites very reluctant to admit that any man's prayer, no matter how insistent, could have any power over the personal freedom of God, but the earlier writers seemed to have considered this the normal way of dealing with Him. And sometimes man did succeed in the contest (Gen. 18:22-32; cf. Mark 7:24-30).

Does this not reflect the real man of hope? Does he not have to contend with God? Does he not have to physically exert himself? And in the end, although chastened by the experience, does he not emerge in a sense as a victor with some claim on God? This does not belittle God's freedom, for He

---

[20]Marshall McLuhan *Understanding Media*. (New York: Signet, 1964), p. 128.

himself has chosen this as the way to succeed with Him (Gen. 32:26-30).

In this E narrative, Moses begins by implying that it is not he who wishes to know God's real name. Rather, God's desire to liberate his people will be much easier if Moses can reveal the divine name to the Israelites. It is the old market trick of telling the seller how much more he will benefit from the transaction than the buyer. We must also remember that, for an ancient, the knowledge of the name of a god gave him the opportunity to importune him in prayer. Furthermore, for the Hebrew, knowledge of the name meant a knowledge of the divine Person. In a real sense, the oral ancient believed he could summon the deity to help him if he knew what name to call upon. Primitive people are reluctant to reveal their true name to someone whom they do not trust, for the knowledge of their name gives the other person a power over them. For the ancient then, the knowledge of the name of the deity, in a sense, gave him a "power" over the god. If the worshipper did not know the name of the god, he could not call upon him by name, and the deity could ignore his requests. Once the god's name is known, the deity is forced to pay heed to the petitions made to him. So usually the god, in the old myths, gave a vague or misleading answer. (Compare the childrens' story *Rumplestiltskin*.)

In this E narrative, it appears that God is not so much concealing His name from Moses, as He is forcing him to recognize the truth of their relationship. God still remains free, and even though Moses and the Israelites will know His true name, that will not give them a determining power over Him. It is a relationship of friendship, and the nation of hope can call upon Him by name and He promises to be "with them." However, they must not think thereby that they can control God. He remains free to answer their prayers or not. In the same way, God wants David to recognize that no single place of worship will limit His presence to one spot. Once David recognizes this truth about the freedom of God, He permits the king to plan to build the Temple (II Sam. 7:1-29).

In this E narrative, as we now have it, God does not at first answer Moses' question directly. He does not reveal to him what men are to call Him in prayer, but rather what He calls himself. His self-designation is not the word which the Israelites would use in prayer; it does not give them the word which will make it possible for them to call upon Him by name for aid. At the same time, this self-designation comes after vs. 12, which is an explicit promise of divine aid in the difficult process of national liberation. The importance for Israel, the nation of hope, is not *who God is*, but *what He will do* for His people. Israel will know His true identity by His future activity among them.

Can it be possible then, that God's first answer to Moses means: "Never mind who I am. You will find out by what I do for you and My people in the future"? Moses had not missed the point; the man of hope knew that God would be with him. He knew that he had been summoned to trust with all of Israel that God had offered them a mutual future with Him. But Moses wanted more; he wanted the true name, so that in moments of despair, he and the nation would know precisely whom they shared this hope with. He wanted the name he could call upon, the one who did control the future, so that he could importune Him in moments of failure. He wanted to know the name of the God who shared his past, his present, and future. He wanted to know who it was who had been with the patriarchs, who it is who is now revealing himself to him, and who it will be who had just promised to share Moses' nation's future with himself. Perhaps a later generation deleted Moses' insistence on learning the true name. However, E had described a valid theological point: the man of hope and the nation of hope which comes from Him need the ability to call upon God in prayer by name. It would be a perpetual sign of the friendship which He offered them that day. And it would give them the ability to face the moments of despair and failure more calmly.

It would be worthwhile to attempt to conjecture a reconstruction of the original E version of this encounter. Let us postulate the manner by which Moses was able to wrest the personal name from the mysterious revelation which had summoned him to lead his fellow countrymen out of slavery and into freedom. The man of hope has gone to a mountain to pray. In the depths of his consciousness, his whole being is suddenly taken over by the Spirit. In the mystery of his own personhood, a voice vibrates with all the power of the divine ruler of men:

*God:*    I am the God of your fathers. I have heard the cry of my people out of their bondage in Egypt. I am sending you to lead them out of the bondage of Egypt into a land which I will give them.

*Moses:*    I am to go to the sons of Israel and tell them: "The God of your fathers has sent me to you. Let us leave Egypt and go into a land which He will give us."

*God:*    I have sent you to them.

*Moses:*    And they will say to me: "Who are you to speak for God? Who has made you a ruler and a leader over us?" For so they spoke when I was last among them.

*God:*    I will be with you.

*Moses:*    And they will say: "What is the name of

the God who has sent you to us?"

God:    I am the God of their fathers, the God of Abraham, and the God of Isaac, and the God of Jacob.

Moses:    But they will not believe me if I cannot tell them Your name. If You do want me to lead Your people out of the bondage of Egypt and into the land which You will give to them, if You are the God of Abraham, and the God of Isaac, and the God of Jacob, tell me Your name, so that they will believe that You have sent me to them.

God:    I will be.

Moses:    If You really will be with us, tell me Your name.

God:    I will be who I will be.

Moses:    Behold, I am only a man, and You are All-powerful. But unless they hear Your name they will not believe that You have sent me and Your people whom you love will not be brought out of the land of Egypt.

God:    *I will be.* Tell the sons of Israel that *I will be* has sent you to them.

Moses:    I know that You will be with us, and that You will protect us from the wrath of the Egyptians, and that You will lead us into a land which You will give us. We know that You are the God of Abraham and the God of Isaac and the God of Jacob. But tell me who You are, that *I* may call upon You in time of need, for then I will be able to lead Your people out of Egypt.

God:    I am *Yahweh (He will be),* the God of your fathers, the God of Abraham, and the God

**of Isaac, and the God of Jacob.**

This conjecture is not meant to recapture the E version word-for-word. The evidence is too meager to make that type of ambitious reconstruction possible. But it tries to recreate the original tone of the E version.

The true name Yahweh is difficult to discover. All the traditions trace a special revelation of the God of Israel back to Moses. E has Moses uncover the essential nature of God in His relationship to the nation of hope: God is *He will be.* Moses, the man of hope, must wait for the future to understand who is being revealed to him. He has to work hard to gain this religious insight: God is the source of promise, the one who will bring fulfillment, the reason he and Israel have for hoping in a freedom which they do not yet possess in a land which they do not yet know. Moses must also admit something about himself in this reconstructed version: he needs the true name just as much as the other Israelites. If he is to be a sign of hope for the whole nation, he needs God very much. Once he admits this to God, he learns His personal name: Yahweh. *He will be* is a revelation like all divine revelations; it conceals the mystery as much as it also illumines it. This is a public, not a private revelation. It is mediated *through* the man of hope, Moses, but *for* the entire nation of hope, and *for* all the people who hope in God as the source of their future.

God's true name is *He will be.* Thus, the nation can call upon Him by name in prayer. But their "power" over Him still remains limited. Israel *does* have a mutual future with God, but since He is *He will be,* He remains free to determine exactly what His people's future will be. He comes into human history when He wills to. God retains His sovereign freedom, and man gains the ability to call upon Him by name. The market haggle is over, and both have won.

This section on The Name of God is part of The Call of Moses (Ex. 2:23-4:9). It narrates the divine commission given to Moses. God selects him to liberate his countrymen from the oppression of the Egyptians. All of his objections are brushed aside: God will be with him, that is guarantee enough that He can bring about their freedom. Moses learns the true name of God and is granted miraculous powers to convince the Israelites of the genuineness of His call. Moses' assent to His divine commission is the beginning of Israel's nationhood. By his cooperation with Yahweh, he led the Israelites out of the slavery of Egypt, and molded them into a nation in their own right with their own worship and their own laws.

This revelation of the true name of God is a grace meant for the whole nation of hope. All who are to be God's people will learn to call upon this name. This is the God who brought Israel out of Egypt, led them through the Reed Sea, and brought them to Mount Sinai. There He gave them the law which made them His people and Him their God. He is thus the God of promises made, promises kept, and promises yet to be fulfilled. He offers them a mutual future with Him. Thus the revelation of God is the key to all of the Book of Exodus, and of the role of Moses in salvation history. For *He will be* is the mutual future which explains the promise, the covenant, the election and the law.

As a man of hope Moses teaches Israel to importune God in prayer. He tells it the true name of God, reveals that He and it together share in a mutual future which began in loving trust. God remains free despite their pleas, and yet their hope remains firm that *He will be* with them and for them. For so He dealt with Israel and all those who hoped in Him in the past.

## The Story of David

After the Israelites arrived in Canaan, they gradually took control of the Holy Land. After two centuries, their enemies, especially the Philistines, had become so well organized that the Israelites had to abandon the practice of charismatic leaders for each tribe. They established a national monarchy which would rule all the tribes and thus make their armies more effective. Saul was the first king, and then David was chosen. He defeated the Philistines, took over the pagan cities, set his capital at Jerusalem, and kept the northern kingdom, Israel, and the southern kingdom, Judah, united. Thus he came to symbolize the ideal king, and his reign the ideal kingdom when Israel was ruled by a single government and shared in a single worship. His reign was later to become a symbol for the Messianic kingdom.

For the nation of hope, its first great king was a man of hope. One faith-story especially typified David as a man of hope who inspired the Israelites to trust more in God than in human strength.

One of their shock-troopers stepped out from the Philistine ranks; his name was Goliath, from Gathe; he was six cubits and one span tall. On his head was a bronze helmet and he wore a breastplate of scale-armor; the breastplate weighed five thousand shekels of bronze. He had bronze greaves on his legs and a bronze javelin across his shoulders. The shaft of his spear was like a weaver's beam, and the head of his spear weighed six hundred shekels of iron. A shield-bearer walked in front of him.

He took his stand in front of the ranks of Israel and shouted: 'Why come out and range yourselves for battle? Am I not a Philistine and are you not the slaves of Saul? Choose a man and let him come down to me. If he wins in a fight with me and kills me, we will be your slaves; but if I beat him and kill him, you shall become our slaves and be servants to us.' The Philistine then said: 'I challenge the ranks of Israel today. Give me a man and we will fight in single combat.' When Saul and all Israel heard these words of the Philistine they were dismayed and terrified.

David said to Saul: 'Let no one lose heart on his account; your servant will go and fight this Philistine.' But Saul answered David: 'You cannot go and fight the Philistine; you are only a boy and he has been a warrior from his youth.'

David said to Saul: 'Your servant used to look after the sheep for his father and whenever a lion or a bear came out and took a sheep from the flock, I used to follow him up and strike him down and rescue it from his mouth; if he turned on me I seized him by the hair at his jaw and struck him down and killed him. Your servant has killed both lion and bear, and this uncircumcised Philistine shall be like one of them, for he has dared to insult the armies of the living God. Yahweh who rescued me from the claws of lion and bear,' David said, 'will rescue me from the power of this Philistine.' Then Saul said to David: 'Go, and Yahweh be with you!'

He took his staff in his hand, picked five smooth stones from the river bed, put them in his shepherd's bag, in his pouch, and with his sling in his hand he went to meet the Philistine. The Philistine, his shield-bearer in front of him, came nearer and nearer to David; and the Philistine looked at David, and what he saw filled him with scorn, because David was only a youth, a boy of fresh complexion and pleasant bearing. The Philistine said to him: 'Am I a dog for you to come against me with sticks?' And the Philistine cursed David by his gods. The Philistine said to David: 'Come over here and I will give your flesh to the birds of the air and the beasts of the field.'

But David answered the Philistine: 'You come against me with sword and spear and javelin, but I come against you in the name of Yahweh Sabaoth, the God of the armies of Israel that you have dared to insult. Today Yahweh will deliver you into my hand and I shall kill you; I will cut off your head, and this very day I will give your dead body and the bodies of the Philistine army to the birds of the air and the wild beasts of the earth, so that all the earth may know that there is a God in Israel, and that all this assembly may know that it is not by sword or by spear that Yahweh gives the victory, for Yahweh is lord of the battle and he will deliver you into our power.'

No sooner had the Philistine started forward to confront David than David left the line of battle and ran to meet the Philistine. Putting his hand in his bag, he took out a stone and slung it and struck the Philistine on the forehead; the stone penetrated his forehead and he fell on his face to the ground. Thus David triumphed over the Philistine with a sling and a stone and struck the Philistine down and killed him. David had no sword in his hand. Then David ran and, standing over the Philistine, seized his sword and drew it from the scabbard, and with this he killed him, cutting off his head.

The Philistines saw that their champion was dead and took to flight (1 Sam. 17:4-11; 32-37; 40-52).

The Philistines had put their trust in Goliath, and he had relied on his own military prowess. Both King

Saul and the army of Israel had lost their hope in God. According to this story, they no longer believed in His promise to be with and for them, so Goliath could taunt them with impunity. He could threaten to reverse the Exodus experience of their ancestors, and he could do it because both he and Israel had confidence only in physical strength. And he was stronger than they.

But David would not accept this. The army of God does not rely on physical strength. It is powerful because God has promised to be with it. And God will surely protect the small shepherd boy who has more confidence in the power of God's control over his future than he does in his own puny strength.

Both Goliath and David prophesy about the outcome. But Goliath relies on himself and his prophecy betrays him. David relies on God and his prophecy comes true. The man of hope defeats the mighty warrior; the nation of hope defeats the army of a nation which trusted in itself.

# Part II:

# JESUS CHRIST: THE MAN OF HOPE

The mystery of the holy Church is manifest in her very foundation, for the Lord Jesus inaugurated her by preaching the good news, that is, the coming of God's kingdom, which, for centuries, had been promised in the Scriptures: 'The time is fulfilled, and the kingdom of God is at hand.' (Mark 1:15) In Christ's word, in His works, and in His presence this kingdom reveals itself to men. The word of the Lord is like a seed sown in a field (Mark 4:14). Those who hear the word with faith and become part of the little flock of Christ have received the kingdom itself. Then, by its own power the seed sprouts and ripens until harvest time (*Constitution on the Church*, no. 5).

### The Jesus of History and the Christ of Faith

The Christ of faith is the incarnate Son of God, the first-born of the risen dead, the Lord of history, and the Judge of all men on the last day. Jesus of Nazareth is the Son of Mary, a Jewish teacher of the first century in Palestine, condemned as a religious heretic by the leaders of His faith, and put to death, as a threat to the stability of the empire, by the Roman government.

If we had to depend on the important people and the humanists of His day for any information about this Jesus of history, we would know absolutely nothing about Him. They wrote about His followers — but never about Him. There is a passing reference in Tacitus that He was condemned to death under Pontius Pilate. Everything we know about Him comes from a small band of His own followers. Like us, they were completely convinced that He was one with the Christ of faith. Thus, they really do not help us construct an unbiased history of the Man, because they wrote only to convince us of the unity between the Jesus of history and the Christ of faith.

This Jesus of Nazareth, even as they present Him, is an unlikely Savior. The religious and political sophisticates of the day ignored Him. He attracted the weak, the uneducated, the rural farmers and fishermen. He was betrayed into the hands of the powerful by one of His own trusted followers. He was abandoned by His closest disciples as soon as He was arrested. His most trusted lieutenant denied Him vehemently on the night of His arrest. He died by crucifixion, the most ignominious death of His age. He died between two thieves and was hurriedly buried lest His corpse desecrate a religious holiday. He had made no impact on the powerful, on the religious leaders, on the political structure, on the great thinkers and educators of His time. He had attracted a large following of the rag-tag poor and the oppressed minority of a small outpost of the Roman Empire. For a while they were caught up in His dream that God would enter their lives and change it for the better. For a while, they too became men of hope. Then He was killed and they went back to their fields and fishing boats to dream no longer.

Save this: some of His intimate followers stole

back into the world and began proclaiming that this Jesus whom men had crucified was indeed the Messiah of the Jews, the Christ of universal salvation, the first-born of the risen dead, the eschatological Judge of mankind. When the pagans said it was abhorrent to their philosophy, these apostles replied that their proclamation was a *wisdom that none of the masters of this age have ever known, or they would not have crucified the Lord of glory.* (I Cor. 2:8). When the Jews complained that it was absurd to claim that a condemned heretic was the Messiah, the apostles answered: *You are Israelites, and it is the God of Abraham, Isaac and Jacob, the God of our ancestors, who has glorified Jesus, the same Jesus you handed over and then disowned in the presence of Pilate after Pilate had decided to release him* (Acts 3:13).

This Jesus of Nazareth may have been abandoned by men, but He has been confirmed by God. He may have been put to death by men but He has been raised to life by God. He may have been a symbol of despair, but He has become the only means of hope. These disciples were belittled, laughed to scorn, driven from town to town. Eventually the Jews excommunicated them, the Romans harassed them and finally put many of them to death. *Be on your guard: they will hand you over to sanhedrins; you will be beaten in synagogues; and you will stand before governors and kings for my sake, to bear witness before them ... Brother will betray brother to death, and father his child; children will rise against their parents and have them put to death. You will be hated by all men on account of my name; but the man who stays firm to the end will be saved* (Mark 13:9-13).

These men did persist, persisted in preaching, and writing, and dying for this belief — that this Jesus of Nazareth and the Christ of faith were one and the same. They kept it up — until they had convinced a large part of the unbelieving and hopeless world that their message was not one of folly but of truth.[1]

They were the first Christian community of hope — an incredibly dedicated group which had no fear of punishment or death because they were so deeply convinced that their Lord and Master had completely conquered death and sin. They could be put to death — He lived forever, and would eventually call back all His own to share in His triumph over despair. Their conviction has become ours to the extent that the letters they scrawled to each other as they raced from town to town have become the foundation of our Scriptures, their hurried preachings the foundation of our dogmas, and their crucified leader our God.

However, though we share with them this fundamental belief in the unity between the Jesus of history and the Christ of faith, we must be very careful not to see too much of ourselves in them. Their problems were not our problems and their way of proclaiming this fundamental union is not always the most helpful way for us to solve the problem.

There is a striking difference between them and us Christians who live in the technocratic 20th century. For us, the fundamental problem of faith is the divinity of Christ and the genuineness of His Resurrection. We readily assent to the Jesus of history and then struggle to unite Him with the Christ of faith. But for the ancient Christians the fundamental problem of faith was the humanity of Jesus and the reality of His Passion and death. They could believe in the Son of God and in His triumphant victory over death. What they found hard to

---

[1]Karl Stern "Thoughts on the Resurrection." *The Catholic Worker* XXXVI, No. 2 (February, 1970), p. 2f

comprehend was that He was really man and that He had really died. The earliest heresy within the Christian community was Gnosticism. This sect dehumanized Christ: they made His flesh into an apparent humanity and His Passion into an apparent death. The orthodox Christians of the first century readily assented to the Christ of faith and then struggled to unite Him with the Jesus of history.

These ancient Christians achieved their unification in their own way, not in ours. They did not look at the past the same way that we do. They did not see their task as that of re-creating exactly the biography and history of Jesus. No other ancients had this approach to history, so why should we demand it of the early Christians? They, like we, had to live and work in their own age with the tools of their times. For the ancients, the past gave meaning and definition and inspiration *to a present situation*. When they looked back at the Jesus of history, they saw the exalted Christ of faith living among men in human form.

For the first Christians, the import of the words of Mark quoted above is not that Jesus once said them, but rather, that Christ is now comforting His community of believers by reassuring them of His compassion while they suffer for His name.

For them, "tradition" did not mean "what happened once and for all long ago," but "what is now going on within the community which has placed itself under the Lord of history."

Too often modern men have approached the New Testament Scriptures with the suspicion that they are being taken in, that the community of believers has played tricks with history to guarantee that we will identify the Christ of faith with the Jesus of history.

Should not the question be: 'What sayings has the exalted Lord placed on the lips of His community?' rather than: 'What sayings did the post-Easter community place on the lips of the historical Jesus of history?'[2]

The Gospel of John is clearly in this tradition. Everywhere in the last Gospel Jesus is the exalted Lord of the Resurrection in human form. He is the Lord of history, the eschatological victor who moves majestically through life to His final hour. He presents His great offering, and then assumes the birthright which was His from the beginning. He is everywhere and always the incarnate Son of God, who has complete control over His own history. He sees through the hearts of men, knows exactly why He is on earth, and what His destiny is to be.

At one time it was thought — especially by Protestant scholars of the last century — that the Synoptic Gospels would be a more scientific and historical account of the life of Jesus. But all their investigations confirmed how thoroughly Mark, Matthew, and Luke were brothers of John: they too had placed the exalted Christ of faith within the tradition of the Jesus of history.

But we moderns have to come to these texts as we are: men who desperately want to distinguish between faith formulations and accurate historical reporting. We need to know exactly what the Jesus of history was like, so that we too can make our own act of hope: which for us begins within history.

Although the first Christians did not share our historical and scholarly acumen, they did see that the only successful way to combat Gnosticism was that they too must start with historical fact rather than with credulity.

The Gospels are the rejection of myth. Rather, these Gospels voice the confession: Jesus

---

[2]Joachim Rohde. *Rediscovering the Teaching of the Evangelists.* (London, 1968), p. 257. Hereafter cited as: Rohde.

the Christ, the unity of the earthly Jesus and the Christ of faith. By this the Gospels proclaim that faith does not begin with itself but lives from past history.[3]

If we keep in mind that these early Christians shared our passion for beginning with history, but did not share our understanding of what history is, we will be able to comprehend what they tried to do as they struggled with the problem of unifying the Christ of faith with the Jesus of history.

In solving the problem for their own day, they created one for us. They constantly put the exalted Christ, whom they understood to be continually inspiring them, into their depiction of the Jesus of history. Thus, when the early Christian would begin to quaver in his faith as the evangelist neared the description of the ignominy of the cross, the evangelist could reassure him by having the exalted Christ predict His Passion and guarantee His eventual victory: *The Son of Man will be delivered into the hands of men; they will put Him to death; and three days after he has been put to death he will rise again* (Mark 9:31).

But how true is this of the Jesus of history? Let us keep in mind that for Christians of all ages Jesus *is* the Son of God, *is* the exalted Christ. But because of the way in which the first Christians conceptualized the purpose of history, the modern Christian is justified in wondering: Is this really how Jesus lived in the world? Did He really have this self-conscious control over His own future? Did He really enjoy this majestic dominance over His own destiny? Did He really completely and fully comprehend His unique role in human salvation? Is

---

[3]Günther Bornkamm. *Jesus of Nazareth.* (New York: Harper and Row, 1960). p. 23. Hereafter cited as: Bornkamm.

there not the problem that if we unquestioningly assent to all of this, that we take Jesus out of history? If we take Jesus out of history, is it not also true that He can no longer be a man of hope like the rest of us who follow Him? If He was truly human, is it not also true that He had fears and doubts about His own future? Like us, could He not have assuaged these fears and doubts by a loving trust that God would affirm His future?

Then we have a Jesus who is truly our brother: one who hoped like the rest of men. And would He not be a most unique man, if hidden within the recesses of His own self-consciousness — never totally clear to Him until His own Resurrection — was the absolute conviction that God *would* confirm His future? Could not the aspect which does distinguish Jesus from us be that He did hope in God when He had every natural and human reason for despairing? Would He not be a most unique man, if He willingly underwent the Passion, not because He foresaw its glorious outcome, but because He trusted His future to God? He trusted that God would not abandon Him — and unsure of what that meant, He said: *Your will be done* (Luke 22:42). Would not a modern man find a true brother here, one he could believe in, one he could hope in? Obviously this is not precisely the Jesus depicted by the Gospels, but can it be the true Jesus of history?

One of the great values of Scripture scholarship is that it makes possible some reconstruction of the Jesus of history. It enables us to study the texts in such a way that we begin to see which community needs demanded that a text be situated and expressed in the way in which we now have it. It gives us the ability to distinguish Jesus' sayings, the community's formulations, the oral and written traditions, the editorial redactions, etc. As we sort through each of these layers, we come closer and closer to what we are seeking: the Jesus of history, the Man of hope.

## The Search for the Jesus of History

Almost 200 years ago Hermann Reimarus showed that a careful reading of the Gospels would reveal that the Jesus of history preached about the coming of the kingdom of God, but His disciples preached about Jesus.[4] If we consider the Gerasene demoniac as an archetype of the Christian disciple, this New Testament account will reveal the distinction more clearly:

> Jesus . . . said to him, 'Go home to your people and tell them all that *the Lord* [author's emphasis] in his mercy has done for you.' So the man went off and proceeded to spread throughout the Decapolis all that *Jesus* [author's emphasis] had done for him (Mark 5:19-20).

Albert Schweitzer traced the attempt of the European scholars of the last century to regain the Jesus of history (Schweitzer, *op. cit.*). He also felt that within the Gospel tradition there was ample opportunity to note the distinction between the community confession about Jesus and the preaching of Jesus.

> The early Church did not remold the tradition for nowhere does it record Jesus giving His disciples directions for what to do after His death (Schweitzer, p. 359).

If this is true, we can postulate that the first theological problem for the early Christian community, to which the evangelist Mark belonged, would have been: How do we unite the Jesus tradition

---

[4] Albert Schweitzer. *The Quest of the Historical Jesus.* (New York: Macmillan, 1922), p. 16. Hereafter cited as: Schweitzer.

which has no claim to Lordship with our own belief that He is the Christ? William Wrede,[5] at the beginning of the 20th century, suggested that their solution to this was "the Messianic secret" in the Gospel of Mark. This device was not needed in the other Gospels whose final formulations were not that close to the Jesus of history. Thus this Gospel clearly indicates the community's conviction that Jesus is the Christ, and at the same time, portrays a Jesus in history who hides this identity. The disciples are told about it, but they do not understand what He is attempting to tell them about himself.

According to Wrede the traits of humility in Jesus' activity on earth are located chiefly in those strata of tradition which depend most heavily on actual reminiscences of Jesus' life, and which therefore still preserve the knowledge that Jesus acted without any Messianic pretensions, hence in humility.[6]

And this stratum of the tradition was not glossed over by the other Synoptic evangelists. Both Matthew and Luke clearly indicate the difference between Jesus on earth and the exalted Christ.

And anyone who says a word against the Son of Man will be forgiven; but let anyone speak against the Holy Spirit and he will not be forgiven either in this world or in the next (Matt. 12:32).

Everyone who says a word against the Son of Man will be forgiven, but he who blasphemes against the Holy Spirit will not be forgiven (Luke 12:10).

---

[5]William Wrede. *Das Meissiasgeheimnis in den Evangelien. Zugleich ein Beitrag zum Verständis des Markusevangeliums.* (Göttingen, 1901). Not yet translated into English.

[6]Heinz Eduard Tödt. *The Son of Man in the Synoptic Tradition.* (Philadelphia: Westminster, 1965), p. 14. Hereafter cited as: Tödt.

The meaning of the distinction is quite intelligible. In the Spirit the exalted Lord reveals himself. He who did not follow the earthly Jesus may nevertheless find forgiveness when following the exalted Lord, i.e., if he does not blaspheme against the Spirit (Tödt, p. 119).

The Christian community now saw the meaning of Jesus on earth and wanted everyone else to assent to their understanding of His earthly life:

> The secret of his being could only reveal itself to his disciples in his resurrection (Bornkamm, p. 178).

So that even when Jesus is portrayed in His greatest abjection, before the High Priest, the Christian community makes it the moment of His great Messianic confession.

> 'Are you the Christ,' he said, 'the Son of the Blessed One?'
>
> 'I am,' said Jesus, 'and you will see *the Son of Man seated at the right hand of the Power* and *coming with the clouds of heaven*' (Mark 14:61-62).

Yet it is difficult for a modern historian to accept these as the words of the historical Jesus.

> We accord with these doubts because it is improbable indeed that the community had at its disposal detailed reports about the course of the examination in which Jesus' words were repeated accurately. Besides, the community was not much interested in historical details, but preferred to describe the passion by means of the words of Scripture (Tödt, p. 36).

At this point we moderns might well give up. If even this Messianic confession is unhistorical, what hope do we have of ever recapturing Jesus as He was in history? It is good to keep in mind that all of the major schools of Scripture criticism admit that there is a genuine historical stratum in the Gospel traditions. They do differ on *where* it is, but they all admit the reality of its presence.

Three important schools in contemporary Scripture scholarship are: 1) Oral Tradition, 2) Form Criticism, and 3) Redaction Study. Scholars who uncover the initial preaching which laid the foundation for the final Gospel texts study the oral tradition. Those who explore the community's theological production within the texts are form critics. Those who try to distinguish the selection of material and summations done by the final editor or evangelist are redaction investigators.

Martin Dibelius demonstrated that much of the earlier preaching was contained in the Gospel texts. He did not feel that the Jesus of history was interested in general ethical norms. Rather, He was more concerned with getting His listeners to prepare themselves for the immediate entry of God into their lives. Since most of the pericopes are concerned with general ethical norms, he feels these belong more properly to the sayings of the early Christian preachers rather than to Jesus.

> When the tradition was created, it was for the purpose of preaching, and the preaching required those sayings of a general character which are probably unhistorical.[7]

When the Synoptic writers tried to "freeze" this fluid oral tradition, he notes that the evangelists

> had a small share in the inner freedom of Jesus, but made an energetic and historically, a very significant attempt to fix the practical value and relevance of the evangelical tradition (Dibelius, p. 65).

By "freezing" the oral tradition at their moment in history, they gave us an excellent opportunity to recover the genuine historical strata.

---

[7]*From Tradition to Gospel.* (London: Nicholson and Watson, 1934), p. 64. Hereafter cited as: Dibelius.

The giant among form critics is Rudolf Bultmann. [8] He has claimed that the historical situation of the Christian community, along with an almost unfettered theological productivity, created most of the Gospel texts which we now have. Almost all present-day scholars owe some of their critical acumen to his investigations. Yet, most of them, such as Joachim Rohde and Günther Bornkamm, have tried to redress the balance by indicating genuine historical strata in these community formulations.

So subsequent scholars have been more careful to avoid banishing the Jesus of history altogether from the Gospel texts. Willi Marxsen, the redaction scholar for the evangelist Mark, reminds us that we should note this biographical presence within the Gospel tradition:

> Our historical investigation of the whole *cannot* lead to a life of Jesus, but only to the history and the theology of the evangelist. On the other hand, *all* reports of the life of 'Jesus' have been transmitted solely within the totality of the individual Gospels; and in their arrangement, but to a degree also in their (trans-) formation, they have been inserted into this totality.[9]

Thus we should not see our search for the Jesus of history as entirely hopeless. It is well to keep in mind, however, that we will not meet a 20th-century technocrat. The Jesus of history is going to belong to His people and to His age.

## Judaism in the Time of Jesus

What was Judaism like in the time of Jesus? The

---

[8]*The History of the Synoptic Tradition.* (New York: Harper and Row, 1963).

[9]Willi Marxsen. *Mark the Evangelist.* (New York: Abingdon, 1969), p. 112, n. 167. Hereafter cited as: Marxsen.

great Davidic kingdom of a united and independent Israel had long since disappeared. The Temple of Solomon, once destroyed, had been rebuilt. The prophets of the heroic age had placed their hopes of a revitalized Israel in the great institutions of their day: the Davidic monarchy and the worship of Yahweh in the Temple. However, many Jews in the postexile period had given up on the human institutions of the kingdom and of Temple worship. They felt that a revitalized Israel could come about only by the direct intervention of God into their lives. They had stopped waiting for the restoring of the kingdom of Israel and had placed all their hopes rather in the "kingdom of God." But this "kingdom of God" had very significant political overtones, for it insisted on the fact that the present rule and the present worship were only temporary measures. In other words, it was the common hope that the powerful of the day would be destroyed by God's almighty hand because they had betrayed His trust.

How did such a view come about?[10] After the exiles of Judaism had returned from the Babylonian captivity, Alexander the Great conquered all of the Near East. There followed a period of cultural Hellenism. Some of the Jews accepted this acculturation, and others viewed it as a threat to their religious heritage. When Alexander's empire broke up, Judah fell to the Ptolemies and then to the Seleucids. The Ptolemies tolerated religious difference and let the Jews worship in their own way. When the Seleucids of Syria took over, however, they imposed Greek customs and culture upon the people.

---

[10]The historical outline which follows is based on "Post-Exilic Palestine" in *The Oxford Annotated Bible with the Apocrypha* (New York: Oxford, 1965) pp. 1527-1529.

Many Jews sympathized with this acculturation, even to the point of apostasy from the Mosaic observations. Some of the ancient writers even hint that such men rather welcomed Antiochus Epiphanes' rededication of the second temple to Zeus Olympius in 167 B.C. They found nothing wrong with assimilating Yahweh God with the head of the Olympian gods. *Forces of his will come and profane the sanctuary citadel; they will abolish the perpetual sacrifice and install the disastrous abomination there* (Dan. 11:31).

But the orthodox Jews could not tolerate such a desecration. They revolted. *Those who break the covenant he will corrupt by his flatteries, but the people who know their God will stand firm and take action* (Dan. 11:32). Judas Maccabeus, of the priestly family of the Hasmoneans, led a successful campaign against the Syrians. In 164 B.C. the temple was purified. This is the origin of "the feasts of lights," Hanukkah. Such a military victory forced the Seleucids to recognize the autonomy of the Jews. For a while they regained religious and political freedom. Judas Maccabeus died in 160 B.C. and the Hasmonean house ruled until 40 B.C. The Jewish Hasmoneans outlasted the Seleucids, who were replaced when Pompey made Syria a Roman province in 63 B.C.

Information about this period stems from the books of the Maccabees, the history of Josephus, and archaeology. Ancient coins are especially helpful in understanding it. Jewish coinage of the time reflects the growing ambition of the Hasmoneans. At first they were content to be acknowledged as high priests and ethnarchs of the Jews. However, starting with Aristobulus (104-103 B.C.), they assumed the title of king. This infuriated the Pharisees, who felt it was a betrayal of the Jewish hope in the restoration of the Davidic monarchy.

The Hasmonean house had to contend with

growing religious and political divisions. The Sadducees, a political and sacerdotal aristocracy, were quite willing to make concessions to the secular tenors of their time. On the contrary, the Pharisees strove to insist on the unique nature of Judaism by close observation of the Mosaic Law. The Essenes maintained their religious integrity by refusing to have anything to do with national life. They withdrew into an exclusive sect which insisted on ethical asceticism. They were an apocalyptic people who believed in the imminent intervention of God in their lives. They could not subject themselves to a king who was not of David's line nor to a high priest of the Temple who was not a pure-blooded descendant of Aaron. The Dead Sea Scrolls at Qumran reveal much of their life-style and teachings. These documents help us to understand the way of life and the preaching of John the Baptist. They also indirectly clarify much about the early environment of the first Christians.

Augustus became emperor in 27 B.C. Syria had been a Roman protectorate since its conquest by Pompey. Now it was made into an imperial province, and was governed by a legate. Palestine was not included in this new set-up, but for reasons of political expediency, it and several neighboring territories were left under the control of local princes. When the Hasmonean dynasty collapsed, the Senate made Herod the Great their king. He ruled from 37 to 4 B.C. Herod began an ambitious building program throughout his kingdom. His chief undertaking was the vast expansion of the Temple. It was surrounded by extensive courtyards lined with porticoes. The Temple was divided into successive sections, starting with the Court of the Gentiles and culminating in the Holy of Holies. One could enter each subsequent inner section according to the degree to which one was consecrated to God.

Gentiles could enter only the outer zone, and to trespass that boundary was punishable by death.[11]

After Herod died in 4 B.C., his kingdom Palestine was given to four tetrarchs. Archelaus (4 B.C.-6 A.D.) ruled Judea and Samaria. Herod Antipas (4 B.C.-39 A.D.) reigned in Samaria. Philip (4 B.C.-34 A.D.) controlled the districts of Iturea and Trachonitis, southeast of Mt. Hermon. Herod Agrippa I unified Palestine. He gained Philip's tetrarchy in 37 A.D., Galilee in 39, Samaria and Judea in 41, and held them all till his death in 41.

During the intervals between these reigns, the imperial legate of Syria directly administered the northern regions, and a Roman procurator had jurisdiction over Samaria and Judea while residing at Caesarea by the sea. The period was rife with political intrigues, betrayals, shifting alliances, sporadic riots and revolts. The common people were dissatisfied with the Roman rule, for they felt that the Jews should be politically free, and that the Herodians were no more than puppets of Rome. There was widespread dissatisfaction with the Temple cult, organized by and remunerative for the worldly Sadducees. Because of this, Herod's throne was shaky, and the high priesthood — which was often bartered for like a secular office — had lost its original prestige.

Jesus was born into this Judaic world about 4/5 B.C. His birth occurred sometime prior to the death of Herod the Great, whom Josephus said had died sometime before April 12, 4 B.C. (Dionysius Exiguus designed the traditional Christian calendar around 525 A.D. and erred about four or five years in his calculations.) According to Luke (3:1) Jesus

---

[11]Herod's political reasons for rebuilding the Temple are detailed in the author's article "Rebuilding the Temple" *The Bible Today.* (February, 1969) pp. 2800-2801.

was baptized by John in the 15th year of Tiberius Caesar. If we calculate from the death of Augustus, this would be 28/29 A.D. Some scholars think, however, we should date it from the association of Tiberius with Augustus as joint ruler. This would place Jesus' baptism at 26/27 A.D.

Luke further tells us that Pontius Pilate was procurator of Judea, Herod Antipas tetrarch of Galilee, his brother Philip tetrarch of Iturea and Trachonitis, and Lysanius tetrarch of Abilene, a region northwest of Damascus. The year of the crucifixion is uncertain, although 30 A.D. is most likely.

The time of the Herodians and the procurators abounds with riots and attempted revolutions against the rulers. Frustrated Jewish patriots haunted the glens of Galilee. Often they were joined by malcontents and outlaws. The people were very angry at their leaders and were ripe for a violent change. The biggest revolt of the era broke out in 66 A.D. against the Romans during the reign of Vespasian. The Jews enjoyed an initial success, but Titus besieged and destroyed Jerusalem and its Temple in 70 A.D.

This was the history of the time of Jesus. But there was also a mood, a way of looking at the world which these contemporaries of Jesus had. We should note several of its elements so that we can better comprehend how Jesus belongs to His own age:

1) Apocalyptic Expectation. Many Jews shared the eager conviction that God was about to intervene in human history in a dramatic and world-shattering way.

2) Compromise with History is a Betrayal. Many Jews felt that the political and ecclesiastical institutions of traditional Judaism had become so corrupt that to expect salvation from these sources was to

betray the holiness of God. Yahweh did not work within history, but outside of it. Things were now so bad that all the pious could do was to hope and pray that from His transcendent throne He would intervene soon and with great power.

3) The Political Significance of the "Kingdom of God." For any Jew to openly proclaim that God was about to enter human history meant that He had finally pronounced His judgment of wrath on the corrupt political and ecclesiastical institutions of the day. No ruler who valued his throne and no high priest who cherished his office could permit someone to preach the end of their power.

4) The Signs of the End. Both within the popular Jewish imagination and within the orthodox teaching there were several signs which would herald this final intervention of Yahweh into their lives:

a) The Coming of Elijah. Elijah had not died (II Kings 2:11-13), and the Jews expected him to return to earth. He would proclaim the coming of the last day, and would anoint the Messiah.

b) The Suffering Servant of Yahweh (Isaiah 52:13-53:12). For the Jews of Jesus' time this did not mean a particular individual, but most probably referred to the nation Israel, which had suffered a great deal, but would now be restored to prosperity because of God's favor.

c) The Suffering of the Just Man (Psalm 22). This primarily refers to David, who was first rejected and then made ruler over all of Israel. It was often applied to the persecuted just man who can rely on God's ultimate favor. Again, it probably applied to the state of Israel. The same may be said of the rejected cornerstone which becomes the foundation of the Temple (Ps. 118:22-24).

d) The Messiah King. The Son of David would restore the monarchy. Israel would regain her hegemony among the nations. Together with this triumphant King the Jews would rule in the new world forever.

e) The Messiah Priest. A pure descendant of Aaron would restore the true Temple worship.

f) The Messianic Age and the Old World. There was a deep feeling that God no longer worked within history. The Messianic Age would not be the work of men cooperating with God, as had been the case with the work of the old monarchy and the old Temple worship of the heroic age. It would be solely the work of God, who would take over human history, which had proved unfaithful to Him. There was no connection between the sinful old world on which divine judgment had been passed and this new era. The Messianic world was to be brand-new and have no connection with human everyday affairs. They were too corrupt to share in this work of God.

g) The Son of Man and the Day of Judgment. This was a popular figure among the common people. He appears in several apocryphal-apocalyptic books. In the Jewish canon He appears only in Daniel 7:13-14. He is the primal man, the creature to whom Yahweh gives the power to judge the good and the bad on the last day. He is concealed from man's eyes, although He had been the first creature made by God. He is always portrayed as the eschatological victor. He comes out of His concealment, sweeps down from heaven, and destroys all of God's enemies. Then He assumes eternal rule over the good, who like Him, are servants of Yahweh.

For the ordinary Jew it was unlikely that all of these figures would be summed up in one man. There was not a systematic development which clearly indicated all the relationships. It was a feeling in the air: Israel had gone through its period of suffering, just men had had enough of the exploitation and power politics of the leaders.

Yahweh was coming soon and with Him His divinely appointed servants. Any moment now they would burst onto the scene and end the old world.

## The Preaching of John the Baptist

During the postexilic period, all Jewish apocalyptic expectation appeared in books and pamphlets. Severely critical of political and ecclesiastical institutions as well as the people then in power, they were never recognized as official Jewish teachings. Daniel was the only apocalyptic text ever to make it into the Jewish canon. However, the amount of apocalyptic material in the postexilic time indicates how widespread this unofficial belief was. Apocalyptic writers often used veiled imagery and complicated number systems to proclaim their message. They knew it was dangerous to be too explicit. Yet they were immensely popular in their time.

> They were men of faith who could see within history, through history, and beyond history the working out of God's triumphant purpose, not only for themselves as a nation, but also for men from every nation who were prepared to follow the way of righteousness.
>
> In a world where evil was in the ascendancy and persecution was the lot of the righteous, they believed in their destiny as the People of God and in the triumph of His almighty purpose over men and demons. [12]

All of these men were writers. In an oral culture, such as existed in Palestine, the public, spoken proclamation of the coming of the kingdom of God would also automatically mean its imminent arrival. For an oral people, what is spoken is what is real

---

[12]D.S. Russell, *The Method and Message of Jewish Apocalyptic.* (Philadelphia: Westminster, 1964) p. 220.

and what is important. As long as it remained written, it was a hidden and secret doctrine. Even so, many knew of it and expected its coming. The Qumran community, the common Jews who were fed up with the compromises made by their political and ecclesiastical leaders, the pious who knew that God would remain faithful to His promises — all of them shared in this ardent desire and expectation of the coming of God's kingdom.

The official postexilic Jewish teaching and spirituality depended heavily on the Scriptures and the Mosaic Law. Teachers commented on their established tradition. No longer did the prophets — those great figures of the heroic age — speak immediately and dynamically to the people as the inspired envoys of God. Rather, the official teachers certified their authority by their knowledge of the Scriptures and their fidelity to the Law of Moses.

In terms of his own time, John the Baptist was not unique because he taught the apocalyptic nearness of the kingdom of God. Rather, his uniqueness came from the fact that he *openly and publicly preached* this apocalypse to the people (Schweitzer, p. 368). Here stood a man publicly announcing what they had been expecting for so long. Such a speaker would electrify his hearers, recalling the prophets of the heroic age, and signifying the end of the world as men knew it. We do not appreciate the startling effect which such a speaker would have on a culture which is primarily oral. In terms of our own time, he can be compared only to a popular political figure. Everyone talks about him as a possible candidate for the presidency. Then one day he appears on nationwide television to announce his candidacy. This is the difference between an unrealized hope and the reality. So it was for the Jews of Palestine when John began his preaching. Whatever his intention, he became a great political force, for he was announcing the end of the established reign of the "men of this corrupt age."[13]

Suddenly Israel had a living prophet! The immediate voice of Yahweh, still for so long, now spoke to His people through one of His holy men. And just as the common people had hoped, He warned the powerful that the wrath of God was upon them. Those who had compromised with the evil age were under His judgment. John condemned them fearlessly: *Brood of vipers, who warned you to fly from the retribution which is coming? His winnowing-fan is in his hand; he will clear his threshing-floor and gather his wheat into the barn; but the chaff he will burn in a fire that will never go out* (Matt. 3:8,12).

Jesus heard of this. He agreed with John's preaching. He expected the imminent coming of the kingdom of God. He publicly joined John. Most probably, Jesus did not preach on His own while John was free to proclaim His message. John was arrested by Herod Antipas and eventually beheaded. His voice was heard no more in public. The people had been his followers, but the powerful had done away with him. Once again, the "men of this age" had triumphed over the coming of the kingdom.

Now everyone was tempted to give up hope. They despaired that God would intervene in human history. Once again, they would subject themselves to the powerful of this world. The great temptation faced them: let us return to "business as usual." Herod had proven his point: you live in his corrupt world and compromise with it, or you do not live at all.

Except that one of John's disciples refused to retire. *After John had been arrested, Jesus went into*

---

[13]For a further analysis of the effect of a speaker on an oral culture, see the author's article "The Word of God and the Mass Media." *Chicago Studies.* (Spring, 1968), pp. 15-17.

*Galilee. There he proclaimed the Good News from God. 'The time has come,' he said 'and the kingdom of God is close at hand. Repent, and believe the Good News'* (Mark 1:14-15).

As a public figure, Jesus took His first risk. He had made a dangerous choice: the message of God is more important than the power of men. He too was going to proclaim publicly the coming of the kingdom of God. He was going to be a man of hope for others rather than a silent assenter to a corrupt society.

## The Easter Experience for the First Christian Community

No one recorded the Jesus of history while He was among men. Therefore, we must understand that before we reconstruct the Jesus of history; we must have a thorough knowledge of the Christian community which did write about His life *after the Easter experience of the first Christians.* We will first look at the early Christian community as described in some of the New Testament texts. Then we will be in a better position to reconstruct the Jesus of history.

The New Testament texts present many challenges to the modern man. Fundamentalists impose a historicity on them which they cannot bear. To clarify this point: Mark creates a "Messianic secret" to explain why Jesus was not hailed as the Messiah during His lifetime. And yet the same evangelist has the blind man of Jericho hail Jesus as the Messiah (Mark 10:46-52). Mark has Jesus go to Jerusalem only once — to die — and yet at His arrival everyone knows who He is. Each of the Gospels is supposed to be written by a close associate of Jesus (except for Luke), and yet they are all the work of Hellenistic Christians with a far better literary ability than the first oral Galilean preachers. Each of them is meant to re-create the history of Jesus, but the ability to harmonize their accounts into a unified biography has eluded centuries of Christians.

On the other hand, modernists try to recover the Jesus of history by conveniently abandoning the *Weltanschauung* of the ancient Christians. No matter how we moderns may feel about miracles, angels, and demons, the ancient Christians did believe in them. They could express the experiences which they had only in these terms. We cannot make Jesus and His disciples into men of our own day. We moderns must take them on their own terms and not maneuver them into our own world. This does not mean that we abandon our critical acumen. It means that our critical acumen must accept the fact that the ancient Christians approached faith in a way entirely different from our own.

Our own faith does not depend on the *style* in which they communicated their message to us.

Theological faith does not depend on this or that human word, on this or that argument proposed to it; it rests on the *veritas divina*, on the word of God that resounds in our hearts and makes us believe. [14]

We must bring our modern faith to these texts, and we must do it in such a way that we respect the tradition which is recorded there.

The Synoptic texts are the point of departure for discovering the Jesus of history. They remain the most valid access which we have to the historical Jesus, but their historicity is tempered by the primitive community's mode of seeing the Jesus event. While the texts are a faithful reflec-

[14]Pierre Benoit, O.P. *The Passion and Resurrection of Jesus Christ.* (New York: Herder and Herder, 1969) p. 328. Hereafter cited as: Benoit.

tion of Jesus' bringing men to God, they still demand a personal faith from the reader. Faith is a response to an historical event, and we need a testimony in order to be able to respond. But we must realize the complexity of the event. The Jesus event always calls into question what we Christians are now doing. Texts which embarass our modern sensibilities nevertheless warn us to be wary of manipulating the tradition to which they attest. The manipulation of historical and social data, which is the core of any tradition, in order to placate modern sensibilities, often is a betrayal of the tradition. [15]

Trying to avoid both a fundamentalist credulity *and* a modern skepticism, let us see if we can uncover the history of the early Christian community and consequently some understanding of the Gospel texts. Then perhaps we will better perceive the Jesus of history.

Paradoxically, the early Christians admitted that their Easter faith began with no faith. When Jesus was arrested and executed, they fled. They did not believe in the imminent intervention of God into their lives. They did believe in the power and cruelty of the "men of this age." So they later attested to a "faith which first had to break down at the cross of Jesus . . . "(Bornkamm, p. 173), but a faith which was subsequently restored.

> Easter faith begins from the objectively established and inescapable fact of the empty tomb (Benoit, p. 259).

Whatever that tomb meant for the Jews and for the Romans, for the first Christians it meant that their faith "was to be rebuilt upon his cross and

[15]Richard Dillon, "Introduction to the Synoptic Gospels" class lecture at Woodstock-College-in-New York, November 10, 1969.

resurrection" (Bornkamm, p. 173). No modern historian can avoid this historical event. No one witnessed the Resurrection of Jesus, but there is ample evidence that the early disciples were *completely convinced* of the truth of this Resurrection.

> The last historical fact available to them is the Easter faith of the first disciples (Bornkamm, p. 180).

And yet the believer has to face the problem of the conflicts within the reports of the Resurrection:

> There is an undeniable tension between the simpleness of the Easter *message* and the ambiguity and historical problems of the Easter *narrative* (Bornkamm, p. 181).

There are certain notes which *are common* in all of them: 1) the difference between the familiar Jesus and the risen Lord, 2) the hesitancy on the part of the disciples to recognize the risen Lord as one with the historical Jesus, and 3) some gesture or remark on the part of Christ to insist on His physical reality and His union with the Jesus of history.

When Jesus appears after His Resurrection, His disciples do not know Him immediately; because of this there has to be a gesture on his part and a

> movement of faith and love on the disciples' for him to be recognized (Benoit, p. 274).

> At the first glance, they do not recognize Jesus — their physical eyes see nothing; they take Him for the gardener or a simple traveler; it is when they believe and their hearts are opened that they become witnesses and the subjects of a spiritual experience (Benoit, p. 328).

The risen Christ took on a special meaning for His followers. God had confirmed what they had lost faith in, namely Jesus' proclamation that God's intervention in human history was imminent. First, He came to Jesus:

What became clear and grew to be a certainty for the Church was this: that God himself had intervened with his almighty hand in the wicked and rebellious life of the world, and had wrestled this Jesus of Nazareth from the power of sin and death which had risen against him, and set him up as Lord of the world (Bornkamm, pp. 183-4).

This divine confirmation gave Him power over the forces which had destroyed Him:

The new cosmocrator in his resurrection and exaltation has entered upon his sovereignty, dethroned the previous rulers of the world, barred fate and the demonic powers from their tumbling ground, and created the kingdom of eternal peace and universal reconciliation.[16]

Their new faith was not so much an assent to what Jesus had taught as it was an assent to what He had become for them:

He who called upon men to believe is now believed in (Bornkamm, p. 179).

And these men now had a new vision of what to expect in the future. They too could hope that God would enter man's history, for He had already entered into Jesus' personal history.

By the Easter event a new light was thrown . . . on what was to be expected in the future . . . (Tödt, p. 293).

So began Christian apocalypticism, which expected the imminent arrival of the kingdom of God. The first Christians believed themselves to live in the final age. God was about to end human history.

The man who understood this shocking event

---

[16]Ernst Käsemann. "Beginnings of Christian Theology," *Apocalypticism* in *Journal for Theology and the Church* Vol. 6. ed. R. W. Funk. (New York: Herder and Herder, 1969) p. 122. Hereafter cited as: Käsemann.

— the execution of Jesus — on the basis of the Easter faith, as a victory, was a Christian. But he who understood the passion in this way saw in the resurrection of Jesus the first act of the final resurrection of the dead. Thus the passion story was also the beginning of the eschatological process (Dibelius, p. 179).

And the Christian was safe, for he knew who the divinely appointed Judge of men on the last day would be:

> After Easter there sprang up in the community the Christological understanding that Jesus himself would also be the eschatological guarantor and thus the Son of Man (Tödt, p. 294).

It is important for us modern Christians to realize that the first Christians believed Jesus had *become* the Messiah at His Resurrection. The first community did not consider Jesus in history as the Messiah but only as the risen Christ.

> At first the belief of the primitive community in Jesus as the Messiah meant this: Jesus became the divinely appointed Messiah at his resurrection, and he will come in the future, bringing salvation. Gradually, however, his earthly life came to be viewed as the life and work of the Messiah — at first with the reservation that his Messiahship remained a secret during this period.[17]

Thus, the first Christians were not concerned with what Jesus had done in time. For them, the most important considerations were 1) the risen Christ is

---

[17] Rudolph Bultmann. *Form Criticism* (New York: Harper Torch Book, 1962) p. 68. Hereafter cited as: Bultmann. The second part of this book, by Karl Kundsin, will be cited as: Kundsin.

one with Jesus our brother and 2) the risen Christ is coming with great immediacy to claim His own.

So the first Christians had an apocalyptic expectancy which depended on their belief in the unity between the Jesus of history and the risen Christ. They too would soon be free from this world of sin and despair, for:

> Easter points to the kingdom of freedom in continuity with the freedom of Jesus (Käsemann, p. 118).

Actually the first Christians did not have a memory of Jesus claiming to be the Messiah. What they did have was His insistence that God would intervene in their lives, that the coming Judge, the Son of Man, would confirm those who were part of His fellowship — in short, that they could hope.

> The Master himself had promised to his own that their attachment to him would be guaranteed and confirmed by the Son of Man. The post-Easter community realized that these words of promise implied a continuity between the one who gave the promise on earth and the one who will come to fulfill what has been promised (Tödt, p. 230).

These first Christians were not interested in gathering together the memoirs of Jesus. They were concerned with an immediate preparation for the glorious coming of the Son of Man. God had pronounced His favor upon Jesus and His judgment of wrath upon "the men of this age." They were as fiery and as fanatical as the other contemporary Jewish apocalyptic sects. Yet:

> The peculiar possession of the Christians was their confidence that in the person of Jesus the heavenly Messiah had already appeared and that thus they were aware of the standards which would prevail at the Judgment (Kundsin, p. 98). They knew the Judge, and therefore they could

hope in their own triumph when the wrath of God
descended upon the wicked world:

> Undoubtedly, the post-Easter community be-
> lieved from the start that the coming Son of Man
> would be none other than Jesus (Tödt, p. 57).

Their world had been turned upside down. The men
of power and influence now meant nothing. Their
hope was in the crucified Jesus whom God had
raised. The poor and weak of the world had triumphed over the rich and powerful. Hope lay in the
coming of the Judge, not in the men tied down to
the corrupt systems of the day.

> What they experience is fear and doubt, and
> what only gradually awakens joy and jubilation
> in their hearts is just this: They, the disciples, on
> this Easter day, are the ones marked out by
> death, but the crucified and buried one is alive.
> Those who survived him are the dead, and the
> dead one is living (Bornkamm, pp. 184-5).

This was all shared by Jesus' intimates. It was a sect,
and their secret was meant for them alone.

> At first the new message had been related
> only as a kind of secret to those within the circle
> of personal intimacy. This was true no doubt at
> the time when "for fear of the Jews" the disci-
> ples gathered behind closed doors (Kundsin, p.
> 107).

But such a secret would have to be shared, once the
disciples began to realize that they were *witnesses
for others*.

> It is possible to distinguish between two kinds
> of appearances of the risen Jesus — appearances
> concerned with recognition and those concerned
> with mission (Benoit, p. 283).

When they saw themselves as missionaries, Pentecost
came to the Church. Obviously, the appearances of
recognition are the primitive community's tradition.
There would be no need to report on a call to

mission from Christ until the community saw itself with a missionary vocation.

Inspired by the Spirit of Jesus, the first Christian preachers set out to convert Israel. Completely convinced that the risen Christ inspired all their utterances, they proclaimed Him openly and fearlessly. Suddenly the land was inundated by prophets! These early Christian charismatics, who worked mostly within Galilee, saw themselves as one with the prophets of the heroic age. Their voice and that of the Lord were one. The living voice of the prophet was the living voice of God. Thus:

> the earliest Christians made no difference between the preaching of Jesus and the preaching about Jesus (Dibelius, p. 264).

As we shall see, many of their proclamations were later put on the lips of the Jesus of history. It is also possible that many of their deeds were also attributed to Him.

> The figures around whom knowledge is made to cluster must be heroes, culturally 'large' or 'heavy' figures like Odysseus or Achilles, or Oedipus. Such figures are absolutely essential for oral culture in order to anchor the float of detail which literate cultures fix in script. These figures, moreover, cannot be too numerous or attention will be dissipated and focus blurred. The familiar practice sets in of attributing actions which historically were accomplished by various individuals to a limited number of major figures . . . (Ong, p. 204).

This would indicate the reason behind the stories of Jesus in the oral tradition which later found themselves in the Gospels as recorded history. For example, the miracle stories in Mark substantiate this suspicion:

> Almost without exception are the miracles of healing and raising performed with the aid of a

miracle-working formula (Dibelius, p. 83).

Thus a modern scholar would suspect that these stories were meant to give guidance to Christians gifted with healing powers (Dibelius, p. 86), who would use the proper formulas in their own missionary work. If this is true, we can imagine the dramatic impact which these Christian prophets would have on their listeners. We could also comprehend how the Jesus of history grew rapidly into a heroic figure with great powers.

> He began to send them out in pairs, giving them authority over the unclean spirits. And he instructed them to take nothing for the journey except a staff — no bread, no haversack, no coppers for their purses. They were to wear sandals but, he added, 'Do not take a spare tunic.' And he said to them, 'If you enter a house anywhere, stay there until you leave the district. And if any place does not welcome you and people refuse to listen to you, as you walk away shake off the dust from under your feet as a sign to them.' So they set off to preach repentance; and they cast out many devils, and anointed many sick people with oil and cured them (Mark 6:7-13).

## The Galilean Charismatics [18]

The first Christian preachers were Galilean charismatics who considered themselves prophets and readily identified with the attitudes and activities of the Old Testament prophets. These itinerants could employ the techniques of charismatic activity. They healed, worked marvels, spoke in tongues, and felt

---

[18]The sections on the Galilean Charismatics, Christian Apocalypticism, and the Q Source depend for the most part on the New Testament lectures given by Richard Dillon at Woodstock College in-New-York during October-November, 1969.

themselves constantly inundated with the power of the Holy Spirit. They avoided taking material provisions with them to emphasize their utter reliance on the Holy Spirit.

These men felt that their charismatic presence radically affected those whom they visited. Their prophetic presence brought peace to the house of the one who received them. Those who rejected them were rejected by God, and they would use the ancient prophets' sign of this divine rejection: the shaking off of the dust of the place from their feet.

They were especially incensed at their rejection by the Galilean cities which had known the earthly Jesus.

> Alas for you, Chorazin! Alas for you, Bethsaida! For if the miracles done in you had been done in Tyre and Sidon, they would have repented long ago in sackcloth and ashes. And still, I tell you that it will not go as hard on Judgment day with Tyre and Sidon as with you. And as for you, Capernaum, did you want to be exalted as high as heaven? You shall be thrown down to hell. For if the miracles done in you had been done in Sodom, it would have been standing yet. And still I tell you that it will not go as hard with the land of Sodom on Judgment day as with you (Matt. 11:21-24).

They felt sure the Lord was coming soon in His glory. They preached repentance from town to town. Those who received them gladly were the "just and holy men." Those who rejected them stood condemned before God's tribunal. They were the "last warning system" before divine wrath came upon the wicked world. To reject their call to repentance was to reject God's final grace. Like the prophets of old, they had a fierce enthusiasm for the coming day of judgment.

They preached only to the Jews. These missionaries were rural men, unaccustomed to wide travel. They rarely visited the urban centers or shared the sophisticated acceptance of the gentiles. They avoided the heretical Samaritans, and *a fortiori* the gentiles. Time was too short: the men of Israel had to hear about the imminent coming of the kingdom of God into their lives.

To bring their fellow Jews to repentance, they preached a reform of life. This reform demanded teaching ethical standards which would enable their followers to win the Lord's favor on Judgment Day. So they taught in parables and aphorisms. Some they invented as the occasion demanded, but it is also important to realize that they also used whatever sayings of the historical Jesus would satisfy their needs.

> The activity of the teachers appears to have been of great significance for the spreading of the ethical tradition. But at the same time, consciously or unconsciously, they helped to preserve and to gather the tradition of Jesus (Dibelius, p. 240).

They could speak this way, for they did not distinguish at all between the Jesus of history and the Christ of faith. The whole brunt of their preaching was that both were one and the same. They experienced:

> an elimination of the historical boundaries between the period before and after Easter (Bornkamm, p. 19).

For them, the parousia meant the great restoral of the kingdom of Israel. They had yet to distinguish between the kingdom of God and the kingdom of Israel. So, they believed that the parousia would come if 1) they were able to restore the 12 tribes of Israel, and 2) observe the Mosaic Law strictly. Thus they would consider any gentile mis-

sion as a betrayal of this bringing about the kingdom of God (Käsemann, p. 112 cf. Benoit, pp.
336-7).

Thus we can see the later tension between the
exclusive tradition which these charismatics exemp-
lified and the universal gentile mission which would
be practiced by the urban, cosmopolitan Jews like
Paul. Both conflicting traditions appear in the New
Testament. There is the exclusive mission only to
Israel: *Do not turn your steps to pagan territory,
and do not enter any Samaritan town; go rather to
the lost sheep of the House of Israel (Matt. 10:5).*
And there is the universal gentile mission: *I want
Barnabas and Saul set apart for the work to which I
have called them* (Acts 13:2) (Käsemann, p. 25).

These men were filled with a "post-Easter
enthusiasm" (Käsemann, p. 106). They did not concern themselves with a historical biography of Jesus
for the future ages. They did not think there would
be any future ages. For them their entire task was to
proclaim the fulfillment of salvation (Dibelius, p.
30). Thus we must realize that these men — who
knew the real chronological sequence of the life of
Jesus — were the very Christian community which
saw absolutely no need for a Gospel. Nor were they
and their historical knowledge to last long, for these
men had absolutely no fear of death. Like their
Master, they willingly accepted the rejection and
persecution which came their way — for to be rejected by such men was to be confirmed by Him.
*Anyone who finds his life will lose it; anyone who
loses his life for my sake will find it (Matt 10:39).*

They had the *Weltanschauung* of *Christian*
Apocalypticism.

## Christian Apocalypticism

The Christian Apocalyptic expectancy stemmed
from the early Galilean charismatics and the teach-

ing of the apostle Paul. For the Galilean charismatics the Resurrection by God of the crucified and
rejected Jesus had ushered in the last age of the
world. In this final age, all secular values were reversed. Man gains salvation not by his human efforts
or by the human institutions which he has created,
but solely because God offers it to him. There is
nothing in man which deserves salvation; it is a free
gift of God.

Thus for them salvation did not come about as
the natural development of human history. The
good men who heeded their message were alienated
from these human institutions and expected their
imminent destruction because they had displeased
God. The triumph of these men — now weak and
powerless on earth, but soon to be triumphant and
all-powerful in the kingdom of God — was the work
only of God. Their own future was absolute and
completely beyond men. There was no organic connection between the present of men and the future
of God, for the present did not have that power in it
to reach the transcendent goodness of God.

As far as they were concerned, this time of God's
almighty intervention was very close — so close that
men would not have time to handle even their
ordinary affairs. They proclaimed two criteria for
the coming kingdom: 1) the *lex talionis*, and
2) eschatological reversal.

According to the *lex talionis*, God would reward
or punish according to their activity on this earth.
*Do not judge, and you will not be judged; because
the judgments you give are the judgments you will
get, and the amount you measure out is the amount
you will be given* (Matt. 7:12). These texts are
readily recognized by the parallel between the
*protasis* and the *apodosis*. *If* you do this on earth,
*then* this is what will happen to you on the last day.

Eschatological reversal, on the other hand, proclaims that the worldly values which are honored among men who have compromised with "this age" will be completely turned around on the last day. What prevails now, will not prevail then. What is weak and ineffectual now will be powerful then. *Many who are first will be last, and the last, first* (Matt. 19:30). *Anyone who exalts himself will be humbled, and anyone who humbles himself will be exalted* (Matt. 23:12).

This eschatological reversal affects all of life. Even the popular proverbs which say such simple truths as "Man can't keep a secret," are reversed. The charismatic prophet claims that it is good that secrets are out in the open. For God has reversed man's secular wisdom. *For everything that is now covered will be uncovered, and everything now hidden will be made clear* (Matt. 10:26). There is no longer a secret sect of apocalypticists. They are openly proclaiming the "secret" doctrine of God's impending intervention. Men want to conceal; but God reverses this, and proclaims that it is good to reveal what has been hidden for so long.

This reversal attitude makes it possible to accept rejection and persecution. It confirmed the apocalypticist in his own vision, for tribulation had long been accepted as the necessary prelude to God's final insertion into history. The fiercer the persecution, the more convinced they were that God's coming was at hand. Let us not suppose that such men were always welcomed as God's envoys. Many were stoned or beaten to death for blasphemy. *I am sending you out like sheep among wolves* (Matt. 10:16).

The charismatics recalled that the Old Testament Jews had heeded the warnings of their prophets and repented. The men of Galilee had not, and thus God would prove an angry Judge rather than a gracious Savior to them on the last day. They would be given the sign of Jonah. The men of Jonah's time repented and were saved from God's wrath, but the men of their time did not repent. Thus the exalted Christ, who had now become the eschatological Judge of men — the Son of Man because of His Resurrection — would come as an angry Judge to them. He would condemn them rather than save them.

It is an evil and unfaithful generation that asks for a sign! The only sign it will be given is the sign of the prophet Jonah. For as Jonah was in the belly of the sea-monster for three days and three nights, so will the Son of Man be in the heart of the earth for three days and three nights. On Judgment day the men of Nineveh will stand up with this generation and condemn it, because when Jonah preached they repented; and there is something greater than Jonah here (Matt. 12:38-41).

They willingly underwent the persecution which these men meted out to them, for it was their only way of gaining admission to salvation. These men possessed an

apocalyptic rigorism which knows no salvation without earthly testing, allows it only to the sorely tried on earth, and therefore proclaims according to Matt. 10:22 and 24:13, the eschatological law: 'He who endures to the end will be saved' (Käsemann, p. 45).

*You will be hated by all men on account of my name; but the man who stands firm to the end will be saved* (Matt. 10:22).

Such were the early Galilean charismatics. Much of their work, their persecutions, and their viewpoints can be glimpsed in *The Sayings of Jesus*, which is a scattered collection of the statements made by Jesus and the prophets who preached in His name.

It now seems probable that some of the prophetic sayings in the gospels were really derived from Christian prophets and were afterward attributed to the historical Jesus (Bultmann, p. 57).

## The Q Source

This source does not appear as an isolated New Testament book, but there is ample evidence of its contemporaneous existence. Paul told the elders of Ephesus: *We must exert ourselves to support the weak, remembering the words of the Lord Jesus, who himself said, "There is more happiness in giving than in receiving"* (Acts 20:35). Luke here records a statement of Jesus which appears in none of the Gospels. Recent textual criticism has also revealed: 1) Mark wrote his Gospel with no knowledge of the other Synoptic texts. 2) Matthew and Luke wrote theirs with no interconnection, but both of them had the Gospel of Mark at hand. 3) Both Matthew and Luke have large "sayings" sections which parallel each other but which do not appear in Mark.

Thus Scripture scholars have argued back to the existence of a collection known as *The Sayings of Jesus.* This would have been composed by the Galilean charismatics, for it contains much of the teaching which we have mentioned as characteristic of them, especially the *lex talionis* and the reversal principle.

The charismatics, as we have seen, made no distinction between their own proclamations and the sayings of Jesus. The temptation to insert heterodoxical statements into these sayings would be readily indulged in by the Gnostics. Thus the whole prophetic charism and their sayings source fell into disfavor with the later orthodox Christians.

In the 1940's archaeologists discovered the *Gospel of St. Thomas.* This document easily explains why the later Christians did not accept the "sayings" source any longer. First of all, the find is called a "gospel," although it is really a sayings book. Further, it was discovered in a concealed place, obviously to hide it from those who would destroy it if it were unearthed. In this text several "sayings" of Jesus could expound Gnostic teachings. To prevent such heresies, the early Christians of the postcharismatic period demanded Gospels which froze the "sayings" tradition and deliberately situated them within the biographical account of Jesus. However, by the time they assembled these Gospels, the actual biography of Jesus (in terms of precise chronology and precise geography) had been lost. They accepted these *Sayings of Jesus* as authentic for the Jesus of history.

Scripture scholars refer to this ancient document as the Q source. It is considered one of the most primitive sources of the synoptic tradition. The major subject matters in this *Sayings of Jesus* source are: 1) The Morality of the Kingdom of God, 2) Missionary Material, 3) The Denunciations of the Hardness of Heart and the Prediction of the Destruction of Jerusalem, and 4) Eschatological Watchfulness.

The *Sayings* source can be seen in Matthew as follows. (Luke has parallel passages in his text also.)

Morality of the Kingdom of God — Matt. 5-7.

Missionary Material — Matt. 9:37-10:42.

Denunciation of Hardness of Heart and Prediction of the Destruction of Jerusalem — Matt. 23:1-39.

Eschatological Watchfulness — Matt. 24:37-25:30.

## The Preaching of Paul

Obviously, Paul's gentile mission contradicts the

exclusive Jewish concern of the Galilean charismatics. However, he did share with them several mutual viewpoints. For Paul, the earthly life of Jesus is not salvific. It is His Passion and especially His Resurrection which saves. For Paul, Jesus is Messiah in virtue of His Resurrection, and not because of what He did while on earth. Thus Jesus is Messianic Savior because God raised Him from the dead:

His state was divine,
yet he did not cling
to his equality with God
but emptied himself
to assume the condition of a slave,
and became as men are;
and being as all men are,
he was humbler yet,
even to accepting death,
death on a cross.
But God raised him high
and gave him the name
which is above all other names
so that *all beings*
in the heavens, on earth and in the underworld,
*should bend the knee* at the name of Jesus
and that every tongue should acclaim
Jesus Christ as Lord,
to the glory of God the Father (Phil. 2:6-11).

Like the charismatics, Paul accepted the reversal principle:

For God's foolishness is wiser than human wisdom, and God's weakness is stronger than human strength (I Cor. 1:25).

He also expected the imminent arrival of the parousia:

Paul knows of an eschatological terminus *ad quem* in connection with the Eucharist: when the fellowship of the Parousia commences the memorial table-fellowship ends (Dibelius, p. 208).

He recognizes the legitimate role of the prophets in the Church:

> In the Church, God has given the first place to apostles, the second to prophets ... (I Cor. 12:28).

Yet at the same time he recognizes the lack of cohesion which the prophetic charismatics are creating in the Church (See I Cor. 12:26). So it became clear later to both Paul and the early Christians that they needed a principle of unity and stability for their community. The prophets, by the very nature of their constant openness to the work of the Spirit, by their refusal to distinguish between the earthly and exalted Christ, by their innate feeling that whatever they said was said by the exalted Lord (and hence by extension by the earthly Jesus), could not supply this principle either for the Jesus tradition or for the self concept of the community.

## The Emergence of Christian Eschatology[19]

One certain principle of stability and unity would be the apostolic tradition. Initially, the term "apostle" does not seem to be limited to the original twelve. Paul uses the term to describe himself, and yet never defines what it means. For him, it certainly did not mean, as it surely did for the later Church, that he had witnessed both the earthly and risen life of Jesus. For Paul called himself an apostle because — and only because — he had seen the risen Christ.

Although Paul was eventually to achieve some type of balance between apocalypticism and escha-

---

[19]The sections on Christian Eschatology, The Synoptic Tradition, and the Gospel of Mark depend, for the most part, on the lectures of Richard Dillon at Woodstock College-in-New York during November-December, 1969.

tology (that is, between proximate eschatology and historical eschatology) (Käsemann, p. 127), nevertheless his central doctrine always remained that salvation came from the death and Resurrection of Jesus. He never saw the Jesus of history as a salvific force. Thus his theological thrust could not serve the later Christian community which was trying to gain a principle of stability that would unite both the traditions of the Jesus of history and those of the Christ of faith.

Why this desire for stability after so much initial theological freedom? Let us call to mind some of the principles of the Galilean charismatics, so as to understand why the Church did change her attitude. Unlike the apostolic tradition, the charismatic prophets never tried to validate their claim to authenticity by arguing back to their knowledge of Jesus. They did not validate themselves in terms of the tradition. Rather, they felt that their own preaching and presence had to be taken as valid by virtue of its spiritual force. Undoubtedly this leads to an uncontrolled creativity. We have already seen what this meant in terms of *The Sayings of Jesus,*

Further, the prophets placed little emphasis on the Passion and Resurrection of Jesus. (There is none of this material in Q.) They did not feel that such a teaching was necessary. They were summoning people to an adherence to what Jesus taught. It is even probable that they did not see these as salvific events, as Paul so obviously did. They held a proximate rather than an historical eschatology. They thought that the best preparation for the coming parousia would be to instruct people just as Jesus had instructed them. They continued to preach the teachings of Jesus about the coming kingdom of God rather than the Gospel of Jesus Christ who had initiated the kingdom.

Also, the Christian Church was beginning to need

a fixed tradition. Whenever anyone challenged the practices of Jesus' disciples, they wanted to have a word of Jesus which they could use to justify their behavior. Obviously, the prophetic tradition, with its constant and continual creative insertions could not satisfy this need. Note in the following selection that it is the *disciples* who are not following the Mosaic tradition. This passage met a community need, i.e., it explained to others why the Christians did not keep the usual fast days. This would be needed by the Christians who were challenged by others to justify their different behavior. There is no hint here that the Jesus of history avoided these practices.

> One day when John's disciples and the Pharisees were fasting, some people came and said to him, 'Why is it that John's disciples and the disciples of the Pharisees fast, but your disciples do not?' Jesus replied, 'Surely the bridegroom's attendants would never think of fasting while the bridegroom is still with them? As long as they have the bridegroom with them, they could not think of fasting' (Mark 2:18-19).

The Church felt a growing need to fix her tradition, to "freeze" it, so that she would be able to meet these challenges with an appropriate response.

As the Christian community realized that the parousia was not imminent, but that they would have to live within history, these concerns became paramount. The Church accepted *historical eschatology* and rejected *proximate eschatology*. She accepted a new tension into her life: that she would have to live a constant dialectic between coping with the present moment and believing in the inevitable coming of the Lord. Once the community saw itself as part of history, then it had to reflect on the meaning of the Jesus of history. First and foremost, salvation was seen, as Paul had taught, as coming from the Passion and Resurrection of the Lord. As the Church faced the noncoming of the parousia, she developed the comprehension that she had to reflect not only on the meaning of this salvific event but also on the man who went through it. Thus she began to see Him too as salvific both in His redemptive act *and* in His earthly life. So the Church became concerned about the Jesus of history.

In this manner, the Christology of Easter underwent a revision. The charismatics had preached the utter separation between the things of men and the things of God. This apocalyptic chasm was now avoided. The cross and Resurrection of Jesus had bridged the gulf between the human and divine. There was no longer a discreet separation from God. Man could live in history and by so doing achieve salvation.

As this doctrine developed, the Church saw herself as a part of human history. This did not compromise her with the world of evil. She was often persecuted, and in her own suffering she saw a need to return to the life of Jesus. To be able to endure her own pain she must continue in time the work He had begun here on earth.

But the memory still lingered that Jesus had not been hailed as the Messiah on earth. The Church, therefore, had to reconcile this with her own present belief that the earthly life of Jesus showed that He was the Messiah. We can understand how this developed if we consider the teachings of Paul, Mark, Matthew and Luke about the Jesus of history. For Paul, Jesus on earth is the future Messiah. For Mark, He is the secret Messiah while on earth. For both Matthew and Luke, He is the evident Messiah while on earth.

We can see the Hellenization of the early charismatic parables in this development. Parables which warn the adherent to prepare immediately for the coming judgment now yield to stories of the miracle-worker. The emphasis is on the grace which comes at the present moment from God. Men are told to accept God into their lives as they live within history. The Church is now accomodating herself to a prolonged stay on earth.

The prophets had lived in an atmosphere of primitive Christian enthusiasm. They had lived in a free tradition which now disappeared as the Church became more structured. Once the Church realized she would last in time, she began to shore up her position. The charismatic roles enjoyed by the spontaneous prophets yielded to appointed offices. One did not preach solely because the Holy Spirit filled him with enthusiasm for the Word; one now preached because the Church appointed him to the office. Inspired endowment now yielded to ecclesiastical appointment. As always, the charismatic saints continued to discipline the institutionalized Church. But now a mutuality emerged, as the institutionalized Church strove to correct and contain her enthusiasts.

Thus emerged Christian eschatology, which announces man's salvation as present rather than as future. But it includes Christian *hope*, that is, the firm conviction that God intervenes decisively in human history. By living within history, man helps God bring about His eventual triumph. Apocalyptic fervor now yields to hope. In this new vision, the Church constantly reminds herself that she has a task to do while on earth.

The moment of grace, the *crisis*, becomes all-important. Keeping always in mind the approach of the Lord in His Last Judgment, the Church yet places her emphasis now on the decisiveness of cooperating with God at this present moment rather than waiting for Him to intervene in the future.

What was said at first only in the face of the

impending eschatological Judgment now gives significance for a lasting period and for the necessary consolidation of the Church in the midst of the world (Dibelius, p. 289).

Preaching dealt not only with the salvation which was to come, but — and this was emphasized increasingly the longer the parousia of the Lord delayed — with the salvation already accomplished (Dibelius, p. 298).

This made necessary a sacramental system and cultic officials for the administration of the mysteries:

At first no need was felt for a fixed organization, with officers and cultic formulae. Even the rite of initiation and dedication of new converts, which was later traced back to the institution of Jesus himself, viz., baptism in the Name of Jesus, only gradually made its way to acceptance, as we may see in tracing the growth of the tradition; it grew up by analogy and likewise to a certain extent in contrast to 'the baptism of John,' a process in which the accession of many members from the circle of John's disciples must have been an influential factor (Kundsin, p. 118).

The charismatics had thought that their preaching would usher in the Messianic kingdom of Israel. Once they had reassembled all of the 12 tribes, the heroic age would return. The Messiah, like David, would rule His people — forever. But now the Church saw her gentile mission as the sign that she was God's people. They had not compromised with the evil world. The true Israel was no longer the political community of the Jews. Rather, it was all those people who accepted Jesus as Lord. The end had not come simply because there were people who had yet to hear the Gospel. *The Good News must first be proclaimed to all the nations* (Mark 13:10).

The reason for the anticipation is that the Christian community understood itself as the true Israel of the Last Days, as the eschatological community — consequently understanding their missionary acting as in its essence no longer pertaining to the course of historical events (Tödt, p. 189, n. 4).

The Church was *in* history and *beyond* it at the same time.

The apocalyptic expectancy of the heroic age thus logically yields to Christian eschatology. Men stop anticipating God and begin hoping.

The consciousness of the immediate inspiration and presence of God, which the doctrine of the Spirit implies, has passed into more or less hopeful expectancy of some return of the heroic age. Christian hope saw that expectation realized in Christ; its experience was the present possession of the outpoured Spirit, given through the Lord, the Spirit.[20]

So the exclusive Jews must accept the reality of the gentile mission, and see it as *the* eschatological sign (cf. Acts 10:37-43).

The interest of the Church and her tradition does not cling to the past, but to today; and this Today is not to be understood as a mere date in the calendar, but as a *present* appointed by God, and together with it a *future* made accessible by God. [It is seen] always as a history which pertains to the present and opens up the future (Bornkamm, p. 116).

Christian hope, its openness to the future, is not a denial of the apocalyptic. It is the realization that the future is in the hands of both men and God.

---

[20]H. Wheeler Robinson. *The Christian Doctrine of Man.* (Edinburg, 1934) p. 74.

After all, apocalyptic is:

> the first Christian view of history, upon which all
> further views will depend. It is the idea that the
> course of the history of salvation and of the
> history of damnation runs parallel, if also in
> opposite directions, and finds its criterion and
> goal in the parousia of Jesus the Son of Man
> (Käsemann, p. 33).

*But as for that day and hour, nobody knows it,
neither the angels of heaven, nor the Son, no one
but the Father only* (Matt. 24:36). If man is free on
earth to do with history as he will, God is free too.
He intervenes when He wants to. There can be no
apocalyptic necessity, no forcing of the divine hand.
Apocalypticists often predicted the *must* of the last
day. They thought they could put a bind on God's
freedom. At a certain point in their build-up of
events He *must* intervene. Christian hope denied this
bind. God is as free as man. God does have a
complete control over the eventual outcome of
human history, and He *will* intervene when He sees
fit.

> The theology of the Church has seen its task
> largely in the overcoming of apocalyptic...
> There is no overcoming apocalyptic with com-
> plete impunity (Käsemann, p. 107, n.5).

It was this Christian eschatology which created the
need for the Synoptic tradition.

## The Synoptic Tradition

Mark probably wrote his Gospel during the
Roman invasion of Galilee and before the destruction of Jerusalem in 70 A.D. The life of the Galilean
Christians during the war years 66-70 A.D. must
have been quite grim. The sanhedrin was on the
lookout for heretics, the Roman courts for traitors
to the Empire. Persecutions, betrayals, and sudden
executions were the order of the day. With all of the

suffering they underwent, Mark's Christian community probably felt the end was near. Their apocalyptic expectancy could well be at its height. But other forces in the community, of which Mark seems to be a member, would remind the rest that God was free to decide if and when to end history. Although there is much expectation of the parousia in Mark, there is also a caution that *first* the gentile mission must be completed.

Matthew and Luke wrote after the destruction of Jerusalem, perhaps around 70 A.D. There could no longer be any hope for a glorious kingdom of Israel. Salvation was not to be seen in the immediate coming of the Lord. Rather, salvation was already possessed in the present because it had been accomplished by Jesus.

> This leads, in fact, to the production of the "gospel" in the literary sense, namely, the account of Jesus' earthly ministry for salvation (Kundsin, p. 121).

The Synoptic writings (including the Acts of the Apostles) are an unusual type of early Christian literature. They stand out as the only historical narratives in the New Testament. Since the parousia does not come with the destruction of Jerusalem, then the Church herself must become historicized. Thus we have the doctrine of historical eschatology: the parousia of Christ does not come on the last day but on the day on which one decides to respond to Him.

The Synoptic texts were not written by intimates of Jesus. Most of these men were dead by the time these documents were composed. The final texts were written by Hellenistic Christians. They possessed the *Sayings*, unsituated parables and miracle-stories, a coherent Passion narrative, Resurrection stories and anecdotes, and the Pauline doctrine of salvation through the risen Christ. What they did not possess was historical scholarship or a chronological sequence to the stories of the Jesus of history. Men of this time rarely traveled widely. Hence their geography was weak and often misleading. The men who wrote these documents were not the sophisticated cosmopolitans of the Empire.

But they wanted to have a coherent story of Jesus. They wanted a text which would put Him in history so that they could freeze the tradition which the charismatics and Gnostics kept expanding. They wanted to attest to their belief that this Jesus of history was indeed the Christ of faith. And they wanted to prepare their own community to live in history — a history often fraught with danger and betrayal.

So they wove all of these elements: the parables, the Sayings, the Passion narrative, and the Pauline doctrine into a continuity which it did not have. In other words, the dispersed Hellenistic Christians who did not have a first-hand knowledge of Jesus' chronology or geography created a sequential story for Him. This "froze" the tradition. Jesus had said this statement at *this* time to *these* people in this *specific* place.

The artificiality of the construct can be seen by comparing the Synoptic and the Johannine traditions. Mark was the first Synoptist to do this, and Matthew and Luke accepted his narrative as historical. (They did edit freely, as a comparison of the parallel Greek texts will reveal even to an untrained eye.) Further, both Matthew and Luke had the *Sayings*. They did not accept the prophetic claim that their sayings were one and the same with the utterances of Jesus. But they did accept the Q source as the actual sayings of Jesus.

The prophets had been willing to die because they felt the Judgment was imminent anyway. Their sayings about this are now converted, and they become the ideal for Christian martyrdom. The prophets had felt the coming of the last day was inevitable. Nothing could stand in the way of the divine necessity. These things *must* come about. But the Synoptists each felt that he had to live in history. Certain things must occur *before* the last day — primarily the universal gentile mission. Luke especially edits out all references which could be taken as the avowal of the imminence of the last day.

## The Gospel of Mark

Mark probably was a Hellenistic Christian writing in Galilee during the Roman invasion. Apocalyptic fervor would have been intense. The Pauline tradition of the risen Christ, the constant emphasis on the coming of the kingdom would have made many eager for the great day of God's final intervention.

Was not the Church suffering intensely? And did not the apocalyptic doctrine teach that great suffering was a necessary prelude to the final hour? But Mark felt that the Church would have to continue in history. She had to see her persecutions as a continuation of the Passion of Jesus. If she was suffering, then she was His true follower. Deliberately, Mark begs the community to realize that the earthly life of Jesus is salvific. They too, like Jesus, will be saved by living and suffering within history rather than expecting God to end history. The reason is that the Jesus of history is one with the risen Christ. Thus Mark becomes the first New Testament writer to forge a union between the Passion narrative, the stories of Jesus' life on earth *and* the Pauline kerygma about the resurrected Christ.

The key to this understanding of Mark is 8:31 which deliberately unites the previous narratives of Jesus on earth with the Passion-Resurrection tradition. *And he began to teach them that the Son of*

*Man was destined to suffer grieviously, to be rejected by the elders and the chief priests and the scribes, and to be put to death, and after three days to rise again.*

His denial of the imminent last day can be seen in Mark 13:8. *When you hear of wars and rumors of wars, do not be alarmed, this is something which must happen but the end will not be yet.* Mark 13:10 goes on to say that the Good News "must first" be proclaimed to the gentiles before the end can come.

Now this "must first" is a Christian addition to apocalyptic doctrine. It is a unique contribution — and the foundation for Christian eschatology. Apocalypticism has always had the tradition of the "must," that is, the inevitable working out of God's plans to the end. No man ever aided this inevitable process. Now something done by men must happen *before* the end can come about. Such a doctrine maintains the severity of the judgment, but it opens the door to the concept of human cooperation with the divine plan. The task is difficult, for men are currently persecuting those Christians who are trying to cooperate with God's plan. As their suffering increases, they are tempted to give up. The apocalyptic doctrine had said that the persecution of the Church would be most severe as she neared her final hour. And the Church might also think — since this particular persecution is so severe — that she is at the final hour. There is, however, to be a long series of such persecutions. She encourages perseverance, not by promising the nearness of the last day, but by reassuring them that they are united with the Passion and Resurrection of Jesus, who will confirm them.

The persecution of the Church does not mean she is near the parousia. Rather it means that, like Jesus on earth, she is separate and holy from the "men of this age" who want to destroy her.

Christians do not help bring about the end by joining in the violent revolution against Rome. Mark's insistence of the fact that the "end is not yet" says plainly that men cannot force God to intervene by arms. There is to be no "holy war" for the Christian community against "the men of this age." Eschatological combat is a different reality altogether.

> If so, the phrase [the end is not yet] would have to be a protest against revolts frequent in that period. They do not compel the coming of the Messiah.

> Due to apocalyptic instruction, it might suppose it is experiencing "the end." It is just this idea which Mark rejects (Marxsen, p. 173).

## The Gospel of Matthew

Matthew used the Gospel of Mark as one of his sources in compiling his own text. By investigating the parallel passages, we can discern a certain amount of editing on his part. This gives us some insight into the theological viewpoint of his Christian community. It also clarifies the evangelist's own perspective. Some of the changes merely indicate that Matthew is shortening the narratives, substituting the language of LXX for the "folksy" style of Mark's Greek, or simply changing common words into a more formal vocabulary. However, certain changes definitely impress the reader as being part of a different theological perspective than the first evangelist's. Matthew does not identify the Gospel with Christ, as Mark does.

> He no longer understands Jesus as the content, but as the bringer and preacher of the gospel (Rohde, p. 125).

> It is clear that [the gospel] and Christ are no longer identical for Matthew as they are for Mark

(and prior to Mark for Paul). Jesus is no longer, as before, the content of the Gospel. He is rather its bearer, its proclaimer (Marxsen, p. 139).

Matthew has included the primitive material which recognized the distinction between the Jesus of history and the Christ of faith.

> We only want to stress that even in the Gospel of Matthew the name Son of Man appears exclusive in Jesus' pronouncements and that Jesus is nowhere made to pronounce that He would be the coming Son of Man. Thus the evangelist maintains the distinction between his post-Easter recognition and the utterances of Jesus (Tödt, p. 93, n. 1).

But because *he* believes them to be identical, he unites the *preaching* of Jesus with the *preaching* of the community.

> Whereas in Mark the risen Lord *now* proclaims his gospel — and thus himself — for Matthew the preaching of the primitive community is identical with the preaching of the earthly Jesus. Hence, it is not he who is proclaimed; rather the proclamation is about him and his instruction to the disciples which have paradigmatic [exemplary] significance for the community (Marxsen, p. 140).

Both Jesus and His disciples proclaim the coming of God's kingdom. For Matthew, this *proclamation* of the nearness of the kingdom constitutes the nearness of the kingdom itself (Käsemann, p. 116). Thus for Matthew such preaching is the Gospel itself:

> This can only mean that *for Matthew the "gospel" is just such a speech complex* (Marxsen, p. 124).

Thus the Church is no longer simply the community which expects the Lord but the community which also must preach His message to men. And it is the community's ability to continue Jesus' work in time which will determine its own eschatological destiny. The Church is in time, and thus also under the Judge of men.

> It is understood quite seriously that the Church is not living in a short interim period, but definitely in the world and that it must prove its vocation there (Rohde, p. 26).

> It is the disciples above all, the Church on earth, who will have to face the judgment (Tödt, p. 69).

Probably Matthew belonged to the order of Jewish scribes. Like Paul, he keenly felt the mystery that Israel had rejected its Messiah and its salvation. He has, however, restructured the old Jewish theology to face this new reality. The Messiah is no longer the everlasting King of the reconstituted Israel. Rather, He is the exalted Lord whom God has made Judge of the living and dead. This exaltation puts Jesus above *all* men and hence all men must hear about Him. The "true Israel" is no longer the nation of Israel, but all those who acknowledge Him as Lord and Savior.

> Only Matthew has felt as deeply as Paul the problem that Israel has rejected its Messiah and its salvation (Rohde, p. 61).

Thus Matthew must distinguish, even in Jesus' time, between the "true Israel" and the "Israel which belongs to the men of this age."

> Whereas Mark describes Jesus as a solitary, misunderstood man and keeps him at a distance from the leaders of the nation, from the people, and even from his disciples, Matthew constructs two fronts. On the one he places the leaders of the nation, Herod and the people, all who belong to Israel, and on the other John the Baptist, Jesus and the disciples, all who belong to the "true" Israel (Rohde, p. 79).

In Mark, the disciples do not understand what Jesus is telling them. But in Matthew, they are one with the Christian community of Matthew's time. They, too, recognize the exalted Christ in the Jesus of history.

> In Matthew, the disciples address Jesus *only* as [the Lord], even in those places where another term appears in Mark; his opponents, however, call him [teacher] or [Rabbi]. This indicates that Matthew has deliberately projected into the life of Jesus the community's confession of the exalted Lord (Rohde, p. 95).

This exaltation has brought Jesus' work among the Jews to an end and paved the way for the universal gentile mission (Rohde, p. 105). But now that the community has taken upon itself the mission to evangelize the nations of the world, more than ever it needed a principle of unity and stability.

James and his Jerusalem community had been too Jewish. Paul, although the originator of the gentile mission, had been too unfamilar with the Jesus of history. There had to be a living bridge between the Jesus of history and the Christ of faith.

> Thus [Peter] became the "witness," without whose authority the "dynastic" and traditionalist tendency of the Jerusalem community, which found its champion in James, could never have been overcome or the unity of the Church maintained intact.
>
> His position of leadership, which at the level of the Palestinian Logia-tradition (Q) is by no means clearly recognizable, begins to be apparent in Mark (Kundsin, p. 136).

This Petrine tradition is continued in both Matthew and Luke. In Matthew it reaches a rigid consistency, which is evident:

   a) from the originally loosely organized common life of a brotherhood of Christian believers to the developed theocratic ecclesiasticism under the "primacy of Peter," with Word and sacrament, a sense of missionary obligation, and a rigid discipline; and

b) from the Spirit-filled life to a teaching or doctrine resting upon scribism (Kundsin, p. 141). The community now sees itself as a Church and Jesus as its founder.

It is not until we reach the period of the Matthaean tradition that we come upon the attempt to trace back the founding of the Church to Jesus (Kundsin, p. 143).

And the Gospel of Matthew is written to be its Bible:

Every group in the developing Church that longed for an ecclesiastical "legislation" and a centralized control, in order to achieve inner unity and strength to resist the hostile aggression of the Jewish Synagogue, rallied about this Gospel. Here, and here only, was it clearly stated that: Jesus himself had been concerned to secure a stable organization of the Church's life, and had not only set forth the fundamental principles of the new ethics but also given rules to apply to the questions of fasting, prayer, and almsgiving; [Jesus himself had] instituted not only the Lord's Supper but also the sacrament of Baptism, gave strict command for the Gentile Mission, and thus himself laid the foundation of the Church with its Word and sacraments. Where, however, further doctrine and ordinances were lacking, he had given to the leaders of the community, in the person of Peter, the authority to provide them (Kundsin, pp. 146-7).

## The Gospel of Luke

Luke, a gentile Christian, wrote after the destruction of Jerusalem. He plainly distinguishes himself from the original disciples of Jesus. He knew both the Gospel of Mark and the *Sayings of Jesus.* He also had access to other sources. Although Matthew's Gospel seems to have been written about the same time, Luke does not know of his Gospel. Passages in these two Gospels which are parallel all depend on either Mark or Q, with few exceptions. Luke distinguishes between the Jesus tradition and the Christ of faith.

But for Luke, Jesus remains unalterably the one who speaks exclusively of the Son of Man's coming and speaks of the Son of Man as of someone different from himself (Tödt, p. 112). The apostles do not preach what Jesus preached. In Luke, they preach what Jesus *did.* He became the eschatological Son of Man by His Passion-Resurrection.

Unlike Mark, he does not want to identify the Gospel with the Jesus of history. Nor does he want to identify the preaching of Jesus, as Matthew did, with the preaching of the apostles. The apostles preached what Luke's Christian community is now preaching about Jesus. This is the Gospel; it is situated in time and it is the message of the Church within history.

When we own up to the development, we see why *Luke's* "Gospel" consistently avoids the noun [Gospel]. He actually distinguishes Jesus' preaching from apostolic preaching. Hence, his work is neither a "gospel" in the Markan sense, nor a [Bible] with gospels in the Matthaean sense but, rather, a "life of Jesus." The time of Jesus has paradigmatic value as the "center of time." It plays a special role and is unique precisely in this role. Of course, the preaching Jesus carried on has something to say to the community of Luke's day, but it cannot be described as gospel and thus not as an element embracing past *and* present. The two are kept distinct. The time of the Church is to be distinguished from the time of Jesus, though both are related and touch each other (Marxsen, pp. 142-3).

Thus Luke is an historian (in the ancient meaning of the term).

An elementary description of the leading motif of the two evangelists would be that for Mark location, for Luke time is all-important (Marxsen, p. 105).

Mark tries to freeze the tradition by setting it in certain geographical places. Luke tries to historicize it by situating it within a correct chronological sequence. Luke follows the order of Mark's Gospel and of Q, as long as it bears an historical and chronological order. He changes the sequence whenever he feels this is necessary in order to create a more definitive chronological outline.

Matthew and Mark had to fit the experience of history into the apocalyptic expectation. Luke has fit apocalyptic expectation into the experience of history.

If, in the other Gospels, the problem of history is a special form of the problem of eschatology, in Luke eschatology has become a special form of the problem of history.[21]

Thus history becomes Luke's overriding concern in constructing his Gospel:

In the prologue indeed he declares the purpose of his book is to give certainty to Christian preaching as far as this can be reached by means of narrating historical facts (Dibelius, pp. 262-3).

In Luke it is not a question of de-eschatologizing in consequence of the extension of time, but of modifying the understanding of eschato-

---

[21]Ernst Käsemann. *Essays on New Testament Themes.* (Napperville, III: A. Allenson, 1964) p. 29.

logy itself. For salvation history as understood by the Synopticist is simply a matter of connecting the historical with the eschatological aspect. This follows from the fact that Luke presents the history of salvation in contrast to that of the world (Rohde, p. 175, n. 37).

But this divine separation from human history works within history through Jesus to save all men and not just Israel. In Luke

Jesus is the center of the history of salvation not as the one who is dying but as the one who is active (Tödt, p. 111).

Thus Luke has a "world-wide universalism" and because he is stressing salvation rather than judgment, he has a specifically Christian concern for the fallen (Kundsin, p. 135). He comes to save and not to condemn:

In none of the sayings in Luke is the Son of Man mentioned as judging or acquitting (Tödt, p. 98).

According to Luke 12:8 ff. the Son of Man appears before God's tribunal as the intercessor, the advocate, the guarantor for the Christians (Tödt, p. 109).

Seeing Jesus as the center of human history, Luke realizes that his community which expects Jesus to be the eschatological Judge of men

stands between fulfilled prophecy and the fulfillment yet to come (Marxsen, p. 196).

If the Christian community must live in history, she must accept the reality of the Roman empire. She cannot make her originators look like men who were rebels to the *Pax Romana*.

So it is that Luke has Pilate pronounce Jesus not guilty, for he is the official representative of Rome.

Both the Gospel and the Acts of the Apostles were written as an apologia, to show the Romans that they had nothing to fear from Christianity, either from Paul or from Jesus (Benoit, p. 143). But the Church still lives in expectation of the coming of the Son of Man (Luke 17:24 and 30-31). Thus the true Christian lives in history but always *watches* (stays alert) for the coming of the Lord.

## The Jesus of History

The temptation now would be to despair of ever getting at the Jesus of history. But one of the techniques of modern Scripture scholarship lets us get as close as we can to this most unusual man. The method is to investigate certain texts which reveal the thought of a *unique and original religious thinker.* Often these texts persist in the tradition, even when they do not fit or even militate against the community's or evangelist's theological needs. Thus, the Scripture scholar argues, these endured because they came from the Master himself.

We must keep in mind Wrede's warning that the first-century Christians rarely appealed to the words or actions of the Jesus of history when they formulated the tradition. This technique was more proper to the second and third-century Christians in their polemics with the Gnostics.

However, we cannot accept a complete skepticism about our present ability to reconstruct the Jesus of history.

Jesus began His preaching by limiting himself only to the Jews. He believed the kingdom of God was near; the time had come for the Jewish nation to accept its role as Savior of the world. Once purified, the people would receive the Messiah from God. Then they would be a means of salvation for all people.

Jesus worked deliberately to bring about God's original plan. This design, announced by the prophets, was the salvation of the pagans *through Israel.* The whole Bible illustrates this plan of salvation. God chooses a people and applies himself to converting them; when he has converted and saved them, he will give them the Messiah in order to draw all humanity to this salvation in their work; then the light will shine throughout the world. This doctrine is set out especially in the Book of Isaiah (see, for example, Is. 2:1-5). Jesus tried loyally to apply this program, to preach to his own people and shape Israel, leaving to later the universal dimension of salvation (Benoit, p. 335).

In the days to come
the mountain of the Temple of Yahweh
shall tower over the mountains
and be lifted higher than the hills.
All the nations will stream to it,
peoples without number will come to it;
and they will say:
'Come, let us go up to the mountain of Yahweh,
to the Temple of the God of Jacob
that he may teach us his ways
so that we may walk in his paths;
since the Law will go out from Zion,
and the oracle of Yahweh from Jerusalem.'
He will wield authority over the nations
and adjudicate between many peoples;
these will hammer their swords into ploughshares,
their spears into sickles.
Nation will not lift sword against nation,
there will be no more training for war.
O House of Jacob, come,
let us walk in the light of Yahweh. (Is. 2:1-5).

Now this message was dearest to the hearts of the common people. At the time it was shared by many of the scribes and Pharisees who were also looking for the kingdom of God. Hence we may note that although Mark does not have them fighting Jesus at the beginning, both Matthew and Luke do. So we may safely state

the schematic representation according to which the Pharisees and the scribes are *from the outset* [author's italics] the sworn enemies of Jesus is certainly unhistorical (Bultmann, p. 35).

The eschatological *lex talionis* which is part of *The Sayings of Jesus* is not original to Jesus. But it most likely is very close to His own preaching: in the kingdom of God there will be a correlation between *present* action and *future* role (Matt. 5:3-10).

*I tell you, if anyone openly declares himself for me in the presence of men, the Son of Man will declare himself for him in the presence of God's angels.*[22] (Luke 12:8).

However, the reversal principle which is also in *The Sayings of Jesus* is most original. Sayings and parables which employ it argue back to the original contribution of Jesus to the make-up of the kingdom of God. Jesus' revolution in religious thought begins here: the kingdom is for those *who have been rejected by the "men of this age."* The kingdom does not come to the powerful but to the weak, not to the rich but the poor, not to the just but to the sinners who need it.

Jesus' special contribution to religious thought is that He combines at once the God of the past (creator), the present (grace), and the future (kingdom). Tradition, present eschatology, and apocalypticism meet all at once in Him.

The power of the future — and only it — can be an object of hope and trust; for the future has

---

[22]This saying, considered an authentic one of Jesus, is both in Q and in Mark. Cf. Mark 8:38 and Matt. 10:33. See Tödt, p. 65.

power over that which is temporarily present and releases the forces which overcome it. Precisely for this reason it alone is capable of both saving and maintaining. Since the future has had power in the same way over the present (*das Vorhandene*) during every past time, everything which has come into being (*das Gewordene*) even of long past times has consequently come into being and has again been transformed anew by that same power of the future which decides about our present just as it is what has produced this present. The consideration of the power of the future over the present leads consequently to a new idea of creation, an idea which is not oriented toward an event in the primordial past but is instead oriented toward the eschatological future. Ernst Bloch has thought it necessary to reject God the Creator in favor of the kingdom as the perfection which has not yet come into being, because he judged God the Creator to be an expression of an 'opulent mythology of the past.' The strong influence of such prehistorical mythology on the manner of thought in the Biblical creation texts is certainly not to be denied. But the God of the kingdom to come would have had to become the cause of an eschatological change in the idea of creation as soon as he — as happened in Jesus' message — had been recognized by virtue of the future of his reign — as the God having sole mastery over the temporally present world and having the decision about the sense and essence (*Wesen*) of the world. In Jesus' message creation and eschatological future are extremely closely correlated. Before now, theology has of course not perceived the problem contained in the message because the theological doctrines about creation were caught in the spell of prehistorical thinking of

mythical origin — in contrast to the eschatological character of the message and history of
Jesus.[23]

For Wolfhart Pannenberg, there is no distinction
between the apocalyptic fervor of the early Christians and Jesus' message. Many other scholars have
felt that the early community misread Jesus' proclamation about the approach of the kingdom. But for
Pannenberg, Jesus was just as apocalyptic as the
early Church. He denies a conflict between eschatology and apocalyptic. Jesus' vision is not of
realized eschatology but of inaugurated eschatology.
His message is not oriented toward what has been
accomplished. Rather, Jesus is concerned about
what is to be done. The task is before us — we must
be future-oriented. We must make the coming of
God's kingdom possible. We must be men of hope,
involved in the task of preparing ourselves for His
coming.

It is a time of grace, a time to respond to *something greater*, God's call to build the kingdom. And
to reject this call of personal involvement in the
present is asking for future condemnation.

Note that in this authentic saying Jesus does not
talk about *"someone greater"* but *"something
greater."* For His disciples, "the sign of Jonah"
meant the risen Lord, but for Jesus it meant *the
very act of preaching the kingdom.*

On Judgment day the men of Nineveh will
stand up with this generation and condemn it,
because when Jonah preached they repented; and
there is something greater than Jonah here.

On Judgment day the Queen of the South will
rise up with this generation and condemn it,
because she came from the ends of the earth to

---

[23]Wolfhart Pannenberg, "The God of Hope" *Cross Currents* Vol. XVIII, no. 3 (Summer, 1968) pp. 290-291.

hear the wisdom of Solomon; and there is something greater than Solomon here (Matt. 12:41-42).

His hearers have to decide for or against God's kingdom and they have to decide *right now*:

> To make the reality of God present: this is the essential mystery of Jesus. This making-present of the reality of God signifies the end of the world in which it takes place . . . A world has come to its end, be it for salvation or for judgment. Its past is called in question. Its future is no longer secure — that future toward which it has been moving, according to all those traditions and laws which have been valid until then (Bornkamm, p. 62).

So the first issue between Jesus and the Pharisees is not *His* person, but *the issue* of the kingdom of God. Jesus preached God's impending sovereignty breaking into the world. He was its spokesman and He pleaded with His fellow countrymen to ready themselves for this divine irruption into history.

Unlike the objective of the usual apocalyptic doctrine, Jesus did not want the Jews to wait passively for God to act in human history. Man was being called to cooperate in this new kingdom. Man was responsible for his present time before God. He must respond to the present signs of the times, he must demonstrate his commitment to the present. He cannot have a false hope that God will make his future. God will condemn him if he does not work for his mutual future with God. This was Jesus' central message. It took the heart of truth out of contemporary apocalyptic doctrine and reformulated it as an eschatology of grace.

The brunt of the parables is that man must prepare for this present role:

> Jülicher has shown in . . . *The Parables of Jesus* that the Christian community and the evan-

gelists have often misinterpreted the parables, for the reason that they looked upon them as allegories secretly setting forth in advance the destiny of Jesus or that of His followers; while the truth is that the parables were not designed originally to conceal anything but to make something clear — by means of a story based upon everyday human affairs or relations, requiring an exercise of judgment in the realm of the spiritual life, with which it is really concerned (Bultmann, p. 48).

The all-important consideration for the man of God is NOW:

> There is nothing in contemporary Judaism which corresponds to the immediacy with which he teaches (Bornkamm, p. 57).

When His listeners asked Him to validate His request that they join Him in preparing for the coming of the kingdom, He repudiated them. To ask for a cosmic sign in the heavens (Matt. 16:1-4) is to attempt to put strictures on God. The call itself to prepare is sign enough for those who believe in God's sovereignty over men.

> They asked him if he would show them a sign from heaven. He replied, 'In the evening you say, "It will be fine; there is a red sky," and in the morning, "Stormy weather today; the sky is red and overcast." You know how to read the face of the sky, but you cannot read the signs of the times. It is an evil and unfaithful generation that asks for a sign! The only sign it will be given is the sign of Jonah.'

What can be said of the man who asks for a sign?

> He is running away from God's call, here and now; he is closing himself and at the same time has lost the future of God by the very attempt to possess it (Bornkamm, p. 75).

Jesus speaks His beatitudes, not as the aphorisms of

a wisdom-teacher. Rather, they summon men to respond to God's call in the present and promise that God will confirm that allegiance to Him in the future (Bornkamm, p. 75). In His parables Jesus is not simply an apocalypticist warning his hearers *memento mori* (Remember man that thou must die!) but He is primarily telling them to seek for the kingdom of God (Bornkamm, pp. 88-89).

Time has vanished before His eyes. To live for God in the present is to be confirmed by God in the future.

> Hence in Jesus' preaching, speaking of the present means speaking of the future, and vice-versa (Bornkamm, p. 93).

Jesus does not abandon His apocalyptic stance; He brings it to the present and makes it the criterion by which man acts in the present.

> The future of God is *salvation* to the man who apprehends the present as God's present, and as the hour of salvation. The future of God is *judgment* for the man who does not accept the "now" of God but clings to his own present, his own past, and also to his own dreams of the future (Bornkamm, p. 93).

So Jesus' preaching always yokes together today and the future:

> It is always concerned with the now and the today in the light of eternity (Bornkamm, p. 170).

Jesus stressed the decisiveness of the moment rather than the approach of judgment. Jesus took:

> his start from the apocalyptically determined message of the Baptist, yet his own preaching was not constitutively stamped by apocalyptic but proclaimed the immediate nearness of God (Käsemann, p. 40).

Jesus obviously speaks of the coming [of the kingdom] in a different sense from the Baptist and contemporary Judaism, namely, not exclusively, nor even only primarily, in relation to a chronologically datable end of the world (Käsemann, p. 104).

For the Baptist, repentance summoned man to God's wrath. For Jesus, repentance summoned man to God's grace (Käsemann, p. 105). The kingdom of God was not coming with fire and destruction; it has already started with God's invitation of grace and man's response.

> Jesus regarded it as his task, and as the special grace conferred on him, to testify to the gracious God as present and breaking into the world (Käsemann, p. 116).

Man now has to learn how to reign — he has to learn to live beyond law and ethics and instead lovingly respond to God's invitation to share with Him the task of ruling in the coming kingdom.

> There is for Jesus no ethic of the kingdom of God, for in the kingdom of God all natural relationships, even, for example, the distinction of sex (Mark 12:25-26) are abolished. Temptation and sin no longer exist. All is 'reign,' a reign which has gradations — Jesus speaks of the 'least in the kingdom of God' according as it has been determined in each individual case from all eternity, and according as each by his self-humiliation and refusal to rule in the present age has proved his fitness for bearing rule in the future kingdom (Schweitzer, p. 364).

What matters is not *this* or *that* law; what matters is are *you* willing to cooperate *right now* in helping to bring about the kingdom?

> Only the future, which is God's, can bring salvation to man; and this future still faces man, in the present, and requires of him the decision for the world or for God. This is exactly the sense that Jesus' moral demands held. Jesus sets

forth neither an individual nor a social ethic; that is, he measured the deeds of men neither according to an ideal conception of human personality nor of human society, but he taught men that the present instant is the moment of decision in which it is possible to yield up every claim of one's own and submit obediently to the will of God (Bultmann, pp. 73-4).

It is not the letter of the law which matters; it is the response to God.

For Jesus, however, the will of God is present in such immediate fashion that the letter of the law may be gauged by it, as the examples show (Bornkamm, p. 100).

God calls to us not from the misty future nor from the transcendent heaven. He summons us now as we are in time through our neighbor who needs us.

Surrender to God now no longer means a retreat of the soul into a paradise of spirituality and the dissolution of selfhood in adoration and meditation but a waiting and preparedness for the call of God, who calls to us in the person of our neighbor (Bornkamm, p. 111).

Piety is not response to law but a response to a person who needs us. Thus Jesus condemns as unfit for the kingdom those who wish to maintain the law but neglect the needs of the oppressed and powerless.

Nor have they any time [for others] in their supposed piety, which neglects nothing among the ordinances and commandments, and yet loses sight of mercy in the welter of their works and achievements (Bornkamm, p. 89).

His hearer is asked to respond to this call to the kingdom not as a Jew but as a creature of God. *Give back to Caesar what belongs to Caesar — and to God what belongs to God* (Luke 20:25).

This means: the coin belongs to Caesar, but

you to God. Probably it contains an even more specific thought: the coin which bears the image of Caesar, we owe to Caesar. We, however, as men who bear the image of God, owe ourselves to God (Bornkamm, p. 123).

The bonds of the law burst open at this pronouncement. Everything that is man's belongs to God — and all men who share in this creaturehood also belong to God. Here is the seed which will make the future gentile mission a necessity for the first Christians.

Jesus *reverses* His contemporaries' exclusiveness:

They treat God as if he were far away when they put the law and the tradition in his place, demand blind obedience, fail to make interhuman relations the sphere of the true service of God, and thus sever the creature both from his creator and from his neighbor. It is certainly necessary to pray for God's coming; but there is no need to worry about it, for God is always at the door in any case.

Our only worry must be not to depart from our creaturely status and not to force others out of theirs. Otherwise, the very God who is near becomes the God who judges, and therewith in fact the God who is distant. If the Baptist proclaimed the God who is drawing near to judgment, Jesus understood — and lived — the gracious approach of God as a judgment upon those who are deluded into pushing law, religion, and theology between God and themselves. In teaching and in act he takes his bearings on the creator and his creature. This means that in practice the torah breaks down before him, and his message tends towards universality in virtue of the fact that it is addressed to the Jew as man in his creatureliness.

> But now in so doing he points in fact beyond
> his own earthly appearances on the scene to a
> future that is respected and held open by it
> (Käsemann, p. 117).

Because the Jews have been called by God NOW to
initiate the kingdom of God, they cannot cling to
the past. They have a new future before them, and
Moses and the past must yield to that new future.

> Even a prophet could not have gone against
> the authority of Moses without being called a
> false prophet (Bornkamm, p. 99).

How did Jesus expect His contemporaries to
accept His summons? We moderns must note that
Jesus' contemporaries did accept Him as a faith-
healer and as an exorcist. He based His request
concerning preparations for the coming kingdom of
God on His ability to heal the sick and control the
demon world. We moderns may balk at all of this,
but the ancients accepted this as real. Jesus' contemporaries never claimed He could not heal the
sick or cast out devils; they fought over where the
source of this power came: from God or hell? We
must also note a unique demonology in Jesus' view
as opposed to His Jewish contemporaries. He alone
has a hierarchized demon-world where all the devils
serve Satan.[24] There is a kingdom of hell, too, as
well as of God. It is the source of man's despair, of
his clinging to the past, and of his fear of opening
himself out to God's future. And Jesus sees himself
in mortal combat with this adversary for the allegiance of Israel.

Those who accept Jesus' message have gained
power over this kingdom. They can no longer be

---

[24]Otto Kaiser and Werner George Kümmel. *Exegetical
Method: A Student Handbook* (New York: L. Seabury,
1967), p. 63.

subject to demonic possession, sickness, or despair. Their faith in God's power over their future has made them whole in the present.

> In the tradition of Jesus' sayings faith is always linked with power and miracle (Bornkamm, p. 130).

Jesus' miracle stories are included in the oldest *Sayings* tradition. Scholars of the oral tradition have noted that this stratum was used mainly for preaching purposes. But the miracle tales did not serve the immediate purposes of their preaching. So the scholars felt they were included because they were actual stories told about Jesus.

> *But in this way the reality of the miracle is proved* (Dibelius, p. 80).

Form critics have objected that these miracles belong rather to the Hellenized community long familiar with the tradition of creating miracle-legends about a god visiting men. However, the oral traditionalists have answered by noting:

> These, however, are not the words and works of a god, but of a teacher (Dibelius, p. 266).

What was Jesus' view of *himself* in this coming kingdom of God?

> Jesus himself had in his teaching pointed to salvation, but he had not expounded what he himself meant for salvation (Tödt, p. 294).

> In the earliest material within the synoptic tradition no authentic saying of Jesus can be detected which would state *I am* the Messiah, or the Son of Man, or the Son of God, etc. Jesus in His teaching *pointed away from himself* (Tödt, p. 225).

Nowhere in this tradition is it stated that the common people had a different understanding of what the Messiah was than Jesus had. When the Marcan text has Jesus warn His disciples not to reveal that He is the Messiah, it is because the confession would be untimely, not that it is a false concept.

Jesus is telling Israel to prepare for the kingdom. Let them purify themselves, and God will give them the Messiah. He does not arrogate Messianic rank to himself.

> Jesus is to be found in his word and in his action, but he does not make his own rank a special theme of his message prior to everything else.[25]

But Jesus *does* see himself as the prophet proclaiming the coming kingdom. He *must* be accepted in this role. On the last day those who have gladly welcomed His message will be confirmed by the glorious and triumphant eschatological judge. Those who repudiated Him will be condemned. *For anyone in this adulterous and sinful generation who is ashamed of me and of my words, the Son of Man will also be ashamed of him when he comes in the glory of his Father with the holy angels* (Mark 8:38). *I tell you, if anyone openly declares himself for me in the presence of men, the Son of Man will declare himself for him in the presence of God's angels* (Luke 12:8). In this authentic saying of Jesus, His self-consciousness of His mission and His complete confidence in His role for the future are startling.

> In demanding this, Jesus utters an unsurpassable claim. No prophet in Israel ever claimed that men should confess Him (Tödt, p. 43).

Now for the Christian community the risen Jesus was obviously the eschatological Son of Man who would come on Judgment day. Why then, does the

---

[25]Bornkamm, p. 169. It is possible that the Jesus of history did not accept the designation "Messiah" while on earth because it had specific political implications for His contemporaries.

text explicitly express a distinction between Jesus and the triumphant Son of Man?

Taking this into consideration, it is surprising that the community preserved the discrimination between the "I" of Jesus and the coming Son of Man. The preservation of the discrimination is intelligible only on the assumption that it was handed down in stereotyped Son of Man sayings of Jesus whose authority protected it from being modified (Tödt, p. 57).

But then what does Jesus make himself to be?

All we can say with certainty is that according to Jesus' own understanding the fellowship which he grants to those who follow him pertains to the coming of the kingdom of God and hence will be confirmed by the Son of Man (Tödt, p. 60).

Jesus thus declares fellowship with him to be the gateway to salvation (Tödt, p. 67).

He thus takes upon himself the power to forgive sins on earth:

When Jesus promises to his own, with legal validity, fellowship with the coming Son of Man, he frees them already on earth from the bondage of sin (Tödt, p. 130).

Those who join with Jesus in preparing themselves for the coming kingdom have already destroyed the power of Satan over their lives. To open oneself out to God and His plan of salvation is to be free from sin.

Those who follow Jesus on earth will rule with the Son of Man in the coming kingdom. For there exists a:

soteriological continuity between fellowship with Jesus on earth and fellowship with the Son of Man in the kingdom of God (Tödt, pp. 146-47).

The historical Jesus spoke most definitely of the coming of the Son of Man and judge of the world in the sense of the contemporary apocalyptic hope, and did so with the amazing certainty that the decisions made here with respect to his person and message would be confirmed at the Last Judgment; nevertheless he did not give himself the title Son of Man (Bornkamm, p. 177).

In order to understand this better, it would be helpful to list the types of Son of Man sayings in the Synoptic tradition and see to what strata they can be attributed:

| | |
|---|---|
| The parousia of the Son of Man | Jesus speaks of Him as distinct from himself. |
| The suffering Son of Man | Jesus speaks of himself. Some feel "Son of Man" has been substituted for "I" by the Christian community. |
| The dying and rising Son of Man | This belongs to the kerygma of the Christian community. At times it is an evangelist's summary of the entire Gospel of Jesus the Christ (Tödt, pp. 215-6). |

The title "Son of Man" expresses both a union with mankind and a tension over and against mankind. Jesus' assumption of the power to grant fellowship with the coming Son of Man and thus forgive sins on earth is also a tension over and against men while at the same time expressing a deep union with them.

Just as Jesus' [power] is a constituting element in all three groups, so the tension over against men pervades them as well. Jesus' full

authority stands in sharp contrast to this generation's shutting themselves up against God, and
this authority makes his followers stand in this
tension too (Tödt, p. 218).

All three types had been retained by the evangelists'
community because *all three types* had been confirmed by Jesus' authority.

Hence we see that the bridge connecting all
three groups of Son of Man sayings is Jesus' full
authority. Sayings concerning the coming Son of
Man promise that he will confirm the fellowship
of following and confessing which Jesus on earth
bestows with full authority. Sayings concerning
the Son of Man in his present activity assert that
Jesus' action on earth with full authority (forgiving sins, being Lord over the sabbath, having
table-fellowship with tax collectors and sinners)
is an activity of the Son of Man. Sayings concerning Jesus' being delivered express that he takes
the passion upon himself in full authority as the
Son of Man; the rising confirms and makes the
community recognize the objective reality of this
authority (Tödt, p. 218).

Albert Schweitzer had thought that Jesus shared
completely with the apocalyptic expectation of His
own age. *I tell you solemnly, you will not have gone
the round of the towns of Israel before the Son of
Man comes* (Matt. 10:23). But the apocalyptic intervention did not take place, and Jesus had to rethink
His own apocalyptic message.

Keim delineates the concept of the growth of
the self-consciousness of Jesus from immediate
eschatology to a more spiritual eschatology
(Schweitzer, p. 213).

This led to a series of scholars who believed that
because the apocalyptic intervention had not come,
Jesus' self-consciousness saw that He himself would
have to bring it about in His own person.

176

(For Werner) the prophecies of suffering are the solution supplied by Jesus himself to the difficulties resulting from the postponement of the kingdom (Tödt, p. 143).

The time of trial was not come; therefore God in his mercy and omnipotence had eliminated it from the series of eschatological events, and appointed to him whose commission had been to bring it about, instead to accomplish it in his own person (Schweitzer, p. 387).

This gives complete proof that Jesus was conscious of himself as the suffering Servant of Yahweh, the Messiah, and the eschatological Son of Man. He was the first to yoke together the suffering Servant and the triumphant eschatological Judge with the Messianic King.

In W. Manson's view it was Jesus himself who recognized the consequences arising from the synthesis of the lowly servant [of Yahweh] and the glorious Son of Man in the figure of the Messiah (Tödt, p. 142).

Manson follows Goguel in assuming the definite path of suffering and rejection led Jesus finally to regard the path of the Messiah and his own path as one and the same. Thus Jesus' consciousness of himself is raised above the stage of a merely prophetic vocation to the anticipation that he himself after his rejection will appear as the glorious Son of Man (Tödt, p. 142, n. 5).

The theory, however, that a *combination* of the individual figures of the Servant [of Yahweh] and of the Son of Man determined Jesus' consciousness of his mission was widely accepted (Tödt, p. 17).

Thus Jesus forces God to intervene in human history:

He does not die that this one or that one may come into the kingdom of God; He provides the atonement in order that the kingdom itself might come. Until the kingdom comes even the elect cannot possess it (Schweitzer, p. 388, n. 1).

This imperious forcing of eschatology into history is also its destruction: its assertion and its abandonment at the same time (Schweitzer, p. 389).

Literal history does not exist for Him; only the will of God; and this is exalted even above the eschatological necessity (Schweitzer, p. 390). This last observation supplies the needed refutation for the above development. It has a seductive force because it agrees so closely with the subsequent Christian community's confession of what Jesus meant for salvation. But it takes Jesus out of history, denies His role as a Man of hope, and furthermore, contradicts all His preaching about God's freedom in terms of the future. Jesus had no intention of forcing God. He did not think that His message had been denied because the intervention had not yet come. He believed the divine intervention would come when Israel accepted its salvation role as a Messianic people. As long as they refused to accept Jesus' call to begin the kingdom of God, it would not come about. Jesus did not present himself precisely as the Messiah or the triumphant Son of Man. Rather, He presented himself as a prophet who was duty-bound to keep insisting on God's call to Israel to prepare for the coming of the kingdom of God.

He could not abandon God's future which was the hope of His people. Again and again He had to insist on the truth of His message: God is summoning us NOW to share in His salvific role for all men. To reject this message is to reject God. No matter what "the men of this age" did, the people of Israel must be true to God's new request. The promised time had come; it was the hour of salvation. Israel should be willing to be rejected by "the men of this age" for it would be confirmed by God. Israel must take upon itself the role of Yahweh's servant, who would be crushed by men but confirmed by God. To bring hope to all men, Israel must face risk.

As the crowds were appalled on seeing him —
so disfigured did he look
that he seemed no longer human —
so will the crowds be astonished at him,
and kings stand speechless before him;
for they shall see something never told
and witness something never heard before:
'Who could believe what we have heard,
and to whom has the power of Yahweh been
    revealed?'
Like a sapling he grew up in front of us,
like a root in arid ground.
Without beauty, without majesty (we saw him),
no looks to attract our eyes;
a thing despised and rejected by men,
a man of sorrows and familiar with suffering,
a man to make people screen their faces;
he was despised and we took no account of him.
And yet ours were the sufferings he bore,
ours the sorrows he carried.
But we, we thought of him as someone punished,
struck by God, and brought low.
Yet he was pierced through for our faults,
crushed for our sins.
On him lies a punishment that brings us peace,
and through his wounds we are healed.

We had all gone astray like sheep,
each taking his own way,
and Yahweh burdened him
with the sins of all of us.
Harshly dealt with, he bore it humbly,
he never opened his mouth,

like a lamb that is led to the slaughter-house,
like a sheep that is dumb before its shearers
never opening its mouth.

By force and by law he was taken;
would anyone plead his cause?
Yes, he was torn away from the land
    of the living;
for our faults struck down in death.
They gave him a grave with the wicked,
a tomb with the rich,
though he had done no wrong
and there had been no perjury in his mouth.

Yahweh has been pleased to crush him
    with suffering.
If he offers his life in atonement,
he shall see his heirs, he shall have a long life
and through him what Yahweh wishes
    will be done.

His soul's anguish over
he shall see the light and be content.
By his sufferings shall my servant justify many,
taking their faults upon himself.

Hence I will grant whole hordes for his tribute,
he shall divide the spoil with the mighty,
for surrending himself to death
and letting himself be taken for a sinner,
while he was bearing the faults of many
and praying all the time for sinners (Is.
    52:14-53:12).

Although Israel refuses this role of salvation in
God's plan, Jesus is its Prophet. He cannot abandon
it, for to abandon it would be to admit to the power
of despair. No matter what happens to Him, He
must be true to His vocation: He must insist that
Israel prepare itself for the coming of the Lord. If it
does not, it will face His wrath.

And if Jesus' message is not accepted, then He must suffer the same fate as the other prophets of Yahweh.

> Jerusalem, Jerusalem, you that kill the prophets and stone those who are sent to you! How often have I longed to gather your children, as a hen gathers her chicks under her wings, and you refused! So be it! Your house will be left to you desolate, for, I promise, you shall not see me any more until you say: *'Blessings on him who comes in the name of the Lord!'* (Matt. 23:37-39).

And if Israel will not accept its role as the Suffering Servant of Yahweh, then Jesus must do it alone. He will remain true to Israel's true vocation even if He has to be the only one.

> Alas for you, scribes and Pharisees, you hypocrites! You who build the sepulchers of the prophets and decorate the tombs of holy men, saying, 'We would never have joined in shedding the blood of the prophets, had we lived in our fathers' day.' So! Your own evidence tells against you! You are the sons of those who murdered the prophets! Very well then, finish off the work that your fathers began (Matt. 23:29-32).

Jesus thus is willing to face death for His message:

> Yes, the Son of Man is going to his fate, as the scriptures say he will . . . (Mark 14:21).

But nowhere in the Scriptures does it say that the Son of Man, the triumphant eschatological Judge will be the one to suffer. In all the texts, including the apocryphal apocalyptic ones, He is always God's envoy who destroys all of His enemies. Is this text genuine? Did Jesus assume this sovereign control over His own destiny? Is this a community confession? Who has yoked together the suffering Servant of Yahweh and the Son of Man? Jesus or the Christian community? Of this much we can be sure: in the last year of His life Jesus went to Jerusalem to confront the people and the Jewish officials with the reality of the kingdom of God coming into their lives. He wanted them to declare themselves for this plan of salvation to make it possible for God to send the Messiah King. He was enough of a political realist to know two things: 1) A military revolution against the Romans and the current corrupt regime would not bring about the new kingdom. 2) He was a tremendous political force among the common people. If they accepted His teaching, it might well spell the doom of the corrupt men in power. Thus the officials would be most anxious to discredit Him with the people. In Jesus' day agitators were discredited by being executed.

Why did Jesus reject a military revolution? Because it was a betrayal of hope. It tried to force man's view of the future on God. Jesus was not to be found among the revolutionaries, for:

> They are obsessed by a picture of the future of the world; and for them the will of God which has ever summoned and bound us is a burdensome chain which must be discarded (Bornkamm, p. 101).

God is not a God of death, and His true children are not those who kill . . .

> because for Jesus the true future does not demand the sacrifice of man . . . that fatal and yet so alluring kind of sacrifice by which man loses himself to a phantom, a mere dream of the future (Bornkamm, p. 103).

Unlike the other Messianic claimants of His day, Jesus does not lead men in battle. He summons them to do God's will. If Jesus was actually condemned for blasphemy, it was not for claiming to be the political Messiah. Rather, it was most probably because He claimed for himself a rank and mission from God: to herald the coming of God's kingdom to Israel.[26]

What Jesus wanted was all of Israel to hail this kingdom, end the age of "this time," and welcome their new role of salvation for all men. Then God would send the Messianic King. What Israel wanted was to continue with "the men of this age." It rejected Jesus' message and God's new role. As always, the Man of hope had to face the men of despair who ever say "Business as usual." *We have no king except Caesar* (John 19:16). Faced with this rejection, Jesus realized that being true to His message meant that He must face death. As a true Man of hope, He did not approach this with the sovereign aloofness of a transcendent deity; He fell flat on His face before God and pleaded with His Father to take away this judgment upon himself. Take Me out of history — as Satan would say: let me be myself: a prophet whom no one heeds. Let me be a man of despair. And the angel who comforts Him is the messenger from the God of hope: stay within history, live out this destiny, trust that God will handle Your future. Stay true to the very message which You have been proclaiming.

> And going on a little further he threw himself on the ground and prayed that, if it were possible, this hour might pass him by. 'Abba (Father!)' he said. 'Everything is possible for you. Take this cup away from me' (Mark 14:36).

And God's last messenger of hope would have to abandon His prophetic mission. He too would merge into "the men of this age." But God's demands are man's only access to genuine hope.

> But let it be as You, not I, would have it (Mark 14:36).

---

[26]Cf. Bornkamm, p. 158 in contrast with Benoit, p. 104.

We are dealing here with real history, a Man really in the world facing the eternal choice between God and Satan, hope and despair, this world and the kingdom.

> How could anyone have dared to invent a scene that was so disturbing to faith — the fear of Jesus in the face of death? This story was handed down because it was true (Benoit, p. 22).

Jesus stays true to His own freedom, His message, and His belief in the kingdom. He has ended apocalyptic dreams. The hour is no longer the fixed end of a necessitated human history. The hour now zeroes in on its proclaimer. It is the moment of decision; the moment when man freely decides to accept God's sovereignty becomes the great hour. Jesus accepts God's sovereignty; He lives out in His own person what He has been urging Israel to do all along. And so the men who belong to this age must destroy Him.

> So the *hour* no longer marks a point at which a fixed sequence aims but a moment which specially and meaningfully aims at Jesus. That the hour has arrived is not realized out of the necessity of the time sequence, but out of the actuality of God's will which reveals itself here and now in Jesus and wins His assent. His accepting the cup is thus seen as a free act (Tödt, p. 186).

The Man of hope does not wait for the kingdom. He actively cooperates in bringing it about.

Judas wants no part of the kingdom now. It is too obvious to him that the "men of this world" are going to reject Jesus' invitation. Thus he falls victim to despair and betrays Jesus into their hands.

What is Jesus charged with before the Sanhedrin and the high priest? He says that if Israel rejects God's offer of the Messianic kingdom then the city and the temple will be destroyed. This is blasphemy;

it ends "business as usual." Why could He be handed over to the Romans? Specifically because He is calling Israel to become part of God's new kingdom? What role does He assign to himself in this kingdom? How does He justify His call to Israel to repent and ready itself for the coming kingdom? He is God's prophet!

> We can get some idea, then, of the indignation of the Jews when Jesus in turn announces that their city and their Temple are to be destroyed. In their eyes it is an inadmissible blasphemy. This is why the high priest is led to the definitive question — Who are you? (Benoit, p. 104).

In the Synoptic tradition Jesus admits here that He is the Messiah. What He probably did historically was to insist that His call as a prophet was genuine, the Son of Man would confirm it on the last day, and that to deny this was to bring the judgment of wrath upon the nation. Jesus is the proclaimer of the kingdom. He warns that the nation of hope has reached its final hour.

The officials of Israel deny this role for themselves. They turn Jesus over to the Roman authorities as the self-proclaimed King of the Jews. Why? Because they wanted everything to stay as it was, and Jesus the prophet was telling them that the time had come to end the world as they knew it. They wanted the God of the past; the God of the future did not interest them. They wanted comfort, and risk was not their wish. Why did not Jesus object to the Roman authorities that His mission had been misinterpreted, as John has Him do? Because the proclamation that the Messianic kingdom would come meant the end of Israel as a subordinate to Rome. Jesus could be charged with sedition. Although He had never lifted a sword — nor urged any of His followers to do so — He was yet a mighty political force in the land. And now He was calling upon His fellow countrymen to hail the Messianic kingdom instead of the Roman Empire. He was urging them to submit to God's will. This may not have entailed an end of the political force of Rome, but no one in power ever believes he can stay in power when men of hope begin to proclaim a change. To change the world as he knows it is to end his power.

> From the beginning it is clear what is at stake in the debate: whether or not Jesus is the King of the Jews... It is clear that the Roman power is going to condemn Jesus for political motives (Benoit, p. 136).

Jesus was not John. He did not express the sophisticated distinctions between the spiritual and the temporal realm which the fourth evangelist enunciated in his scene of the confrontation with Pilate. Jesus was an activist; He was a spiritual teacher and prophet in a land which always associated spiritual renewal with its political destiny. Was not the Messiah a regal figure? Why did Jesus simply say He was not that King? What He did tell Rome most probably was that He firmly believed that the time of the kingdom of God had come. Rome was under God's scrutiny as well. The time had come for all men to admit the spiritual hegemony of Israel and to seek their salvation from the coming Messiah. What the Roman authorities saw and heard was not a prophet but a political agitator — intensely popular with the common people — who told them their rule was now under divine judgment. Jesus remained true to His message, realizing that in so doing He was sealing His own death warrant.

The Passion narrative contains a wealth of material not only because of the religious intent which it served, but also because there were numerous facts to record. (Bornkamm, p. 155). There is ample evidence that the earliest form in Mark goes back to eyewitnesses or at least to the first disciples. Alone among the Gospel pericopes, Mark is a *connective* narrative. There is no artificial construct of geography or time to argue to subsequent accretions. Mark's Passion story — because of its early composition as a connective narrative — differs from the Gospel tradition as a whole, and this sets it apart from the rest of the Synoptic material (cf. Dibelius, p. 180).

And the only one who could record such a grim incident was one who believed it was part of God's plan of salvation.

> What happened at Jerusalem at that time must have been so offensive and ignominious that a record of these things could seem only a document of shame and disgrace. Only if one was convinced not only that Christ lived with the Father, but also that the disgrace of the arrest and the torture of the crucifixion had taken place in accordance with God's will — only then could the record be made with any meaning (Dibelius, p. 184).

Jesus died on the cross, repudiated by His own people who wanted no part in His proclamation of the coming of God's kingdom. The poor and oppressed returned home, returned to despair. The Man of hope had been killed by the "men of this age." We must forget our dreams of a better world; sin and despair always win out in the end; better never to have prayed for the kingdom at all than to suffer so.

Jesus cried out in anguish before His death: *My God, my God why have you deserted me?* (Mark 15:34). Some have taken this as Jesus' final cry of despair. But rather, it is the beginning of Psalm 22 in which the persecuted just man cries out to God, who in the end does aid him.

But in no sense did this cry express a doubting sense of abandonment, for to quote from the Bible is always a proof of faith (Dibelius, p. 194). Jesus remained true to himself and His message. And the men of "this age" stayed subservient to despair and "things as they are." God was not going to intervene in their lives! Let us keep both apart — God in His heaven, man in his world. Where they intersect, there is hope, risk, and the creature subordinating himself to God's future. Men would rather live with the familiar than admit that God could change their lives for a better world.

*A darkness came over the whole land* (Luke 23:44).

## The Empty Tomb

But God would not let the message of Jesus die, nor even His person. He who remained true to God's kingdom became Messianic King. He who waited in confidence for the coming of the Son of Man himself became the Judge of nations. And He who was the Man of hope for others became the living eternal reason why all men hope.

If indeed Jesus went to Jerusalem in order to confront the city and the Jewish authorities with the necessity of declaring themselves for the coming reign of God, and if he was finally crucified by reason of the decision that this summons was unauthorized, then the central meaning of the resurrection might well have been understood as the authorization of Jesus' message and person by God (Tödt, p. 252, n. 4).

The disciples who went back to Emmaus had given up. There was to be no kingdom of God. Jesus appeared to them and rekindled their hope. This is not a time for despair — you have forgotten that God is true to His promises. The kingdom begins with the risen Christ, continues with you, and goes on until all is ready for the Father (Luke 24:13-35).

Peter went back to fishing; it was the world he knew, safe and sound. But Jesus came to him in His risen glory and forced him to become a man of hope. Confirm your brethren, stay true to my teaching, build up the community of hope (John 21:1-23).

# Part III

# THE CHRISTIAN COMMUNITY:

# THE PEOPLE OF HOPE

When Jesus rose up again after suffering death on the cross for mankind, he manifested that he had been appointed Lord, Messiah, and Priest forever and he poured out on his disciples the Spirit promised by the Father. The Church, consequently, equipped with the gifts of her Founder and faithfully guarding his precepts of charity, humility, and self-sacrifice, receives the mission to proclaim and to establish among all peoples the kingdom of Christ and of God. She becomes on earth the initial budding forth of that kingdom. While she slowly grows, the Church strains toward the consummation of the kingdom and, with all her strength, hopes and desires to be united in glory with her King (*Constitution on the Church*, no. 5).

In the first century the Christian community had to answer three important questions: 1) Who is Jesus Christ? 2) Who are we who follow Him? 3) How do we approach those others, the world, which does not follow Christ? These questions still challenge us today. The answers which the first-century Christians proposed for these problems formed the foundation for our own faith. But they formulated their answers to correspond to their own world and their own contemporaries. Therefore, while respecting their heritage, we too must be willing to face these questions. We too must answer them in a way which will speak to our own contemporaries.

The third part of this book intends to explore the answers given by some of the first-century Christians and at the same time certain contemporary answers to the same questions. What is the meaning of Christ for the Christian community? How does the answer to this question affect the community's own self-identity?

Part II has explored a possible answer to the question: how did Jesus regard himself? It stated that, while still in history, Jesus looked upon himself as a servant-prophet. He understood that He had been personally summoned by the Father. He had to proclaim the imminent advent of the kingdom of God to men. He cleansed the Temple and preached a reform of personal life, for He believed that His country Israel must immediately prepare itself for a new role. Now was the time of purification, for Israel was meant to be a sign of salvation for all men. For Him, sin, despair, and the Roman occupation meant nothing. They no longer had any power over His fellow countrymen. The all-important "time of decision" had arrived. The only important fact was the kingdom of God coming with great power and force into the history of men. Every other consideration had to be swept aside to prepare for it.

Jesus is the first man in history to act as if sin and death were powerless in His own life. His own hope in the Father was all-inclusive. His whole personality was permeated with His hope in God's control over His future. He trusted so much in God that He refused to accept the powers of any force which would hinder the arrival of the kingdom. He recognized sin and death as *real*, but regarded them as completely powerless before the onslaught of God's kingdom. Because God's kingdom was breaking into human history, neither sin nor death could have any claim over man. Jesus literally did not know the meaning of despair; He knew sorrow and suffering, but not despair.

Israel refused to acknowledge the truth of Jesus' message. True to His own self-concept of His vocation, He freely decided that He himself must remain loyal to His message. He had to hope in God's control over the nation's future, although everyone else around Him no longer accepted it. The nation of hope abandoned the Man of hope and its own role in human history. But Jesus remained the Man of hope *par excellence.* He trusted in God's control over His own future. He trusted so much in this that He had no fear whatsoever about man's ability to end His life. He went to His death with this confidence. Jesus did not believe in the power of death; He trusted in the power of God over His own future.

His Resurrection was an attestation from God that this is precisely what man is supposed to be: a creature who hopes more in God than in himself. He must have more trust in God than in the powers of this world. His Resurrection revealed that God approved of Jesus' concept of hope, confirmed it, and confounded those men of despair who trusted more in the powers of sin and death than in the future of God's kingdom which brings grace and life.

Now that Jesus is outside of human history, is it possible to explore the risen Lord's consciousness of himself? We cannot possibly answer this for He now lives in the fullness of the Father's light. Who of us can penetrate such a consciousness? But we can grasp how the Christians of the first-century understood Christ. Through their eyes, we can begin to glimpse something of the risen Lord's own self-consciousness.

The best account of the development of the Christologies of the first-century Christians appears in Luke's Acts. Luke's compositions give us an opportunity to explore the Christology current in his own Christian community and also to study certain Christologies which predate his own work. Thus study will help us to understand how the Christian community, by trying to come to terms with the meaning of Christ for its members, eventually conceived of itself as a people of hope.

## The Meaning of Christ for the Early Christian Communities

The sermons attributed to the apostles Peter and Paul in Acts summarize the kerygma (preaching) of the first Christian communities about Jesus. Most New Testament scholars do not consider these discourses to be exact duplications of the preaching of Peter or Paul. Luke presents them in traditional Greek oratorical style. This type of rhetoric would be familiar to his gentile audience, but it would be too formal and too Greek to come from the earliest Jewish preachers. Secondly, the discourses attributed to Paul do not coincide exactly with the Christology which he presents in his epistles. Thirdly, they contain exact literary citations from LXX. But the first Jewish preachers relied on their less precise memory of the Jewish text. So these discourses are Lucan compositions. Yet they do contain catechetical blocks of material which pre-date Luke. For these catechetical formulations had become so fixed in his own Christian community that Luke did not feel free to alter them. We can understand this more fully when we realize that not every one of the Christologies in these discourses agrees completely with Luke's own understanding of Christ. Luke's own view is revealed in his editorial handling of the material. For Luke, Jesus is the Christ from the time of His birth. Earlier Christologies had Jesus become the Christ: 1) at His parousia, 2) at His exaltation, 3) at His baptism. A careful scrutiny of these discourses, then, will reveal the pre-Lucan kerygma of the earlier Christian communities. Thus we can reconstruct their Christology and their self-identity.[1]

The major divisions of the New Testament Christologies are: 1) The Palestinian Christian community, stage one. 2) The Palestinian Christian community, stage two. 3) The Hellenistic Jewish mission. 4) The gentile mission. For each group the first Jewish preachers had to solve the problem: what would be a meaningful way of proclaiming Christ to them? From this preaching each Christian community then formulated its own understanding of the answer to the question: "Who is Christ?"

During stage one, the Palestinian Christian community believed that God had worked through Jesus' earthly ministry. They did not see His death

---

[1]The material which follows depends for the most part on the lectures given by Edward Mally, S.J. on "the Mystery of Christ" at Woodstock-in-New York during Spring, 1970, and Reginald Fuller *Foundations of New Testament Christology* (New York: Scribner, 1965), pp. 19-20. See also the appendix of Fuller's book on the stages of development in Christology, and his scripture index for the passages cited from Acts.

as a good, but as "the crime of the Jews." They felt the Jews had betrayed His summons to cooperate with the coming of the kingdom. God validated Jesus' summons by raising Him from the dead. Now there is a period of inactive waiting on the part of Jesus until He comes at His parousia, bringing the kingdom with Him. They expect this coming to be very soon. The Christian community burns with apocalyptic fervor.

The story in Acts of Peter and John curing the lame man at the temple contains the Christology of this community:

> Everyone came running towards them in great excitement, to the Portico of Solomon, as it is called, where the man was still clinging to Peter and John. When Peter saw the people he addressed them: 'Why are you so surprised at this? Why are you staring at us as though we had made this man walk by our own power of holiness? You are Israelites, and it is the God of Abraham, Isaac, and Jacob, the God of our ancestors, who has glorified his servant Jesus, the same Jesus you handed over and then disowned in the presence of Pilate after Pilate had decided to release him. It was you who accused the Holy One, the Just One, you who demanded the reprieve of a murderer while you killed the prince of life. God, however, raised him from the dead, and to that fact we are the witnesses; and it is the name of Jesus which, through our faith in it, has brought back the strength of this man whom you see here and who is well known to you. It is faith in that name that has restored this man to health, as you can all see.
>
> 'Now I know, brothers, that neither you nor your leaders had any idea what you were really doing; this was the way God carried out what he

had foretold, when he said through all his prophets that his Christ would suffer. Now you must repent and turn to God, so that your sins may be wiped out, and so that the Lord may send the time of comfort. Then he will send you the Christ he has predestined, that is Jesus, whom heaven must keep till the universal restoration comes which God proclaimed, speaking through his holy prophets. Moses, for example, said: "The Lord will raise up a prophet like myself for you, from among your own brothers; you must listen to whatever he tells you. The man who does not listen to that prophet is to be cut off from the people." In fact, all the prophets that have ever spoken, from Samuel onwards, have predicted these days.

'You are the heirs of the prophets, the heirs of the covenant God made with our ancestors when he told Abraham: "in your offspring all the families of the earth will be blessed." It was for you in the first place that God raised up his servant and sent him to bless you by turning everyone of you from your wicked ways' (Acts. 3:11-26).

Some of these statements come from stage one of the Palestinian Christian community. Peter describes Jesus as the Mosaic servant-prophet during His earthly ministry. This seems close to Jesus' own self-consciousness. For this community, Jesus is the New Moses. The modifiers "Holy" and "Just" are traditional adjectives used by the Jews to describe the prophet Moses. In this speech, Peter depicts God as responsible for everything in the life of Jesus, but *not* His death. Rather, Jesus' death is the work of wicked men who "killed" Him. This kerygma has nothing to say about what Jesus was *before* His earthly life. It does not explain what He is doing during His exalted state. He simply waits until He will become the Christ at His parousia, when God will send Him back into human history.

During stage two, the Palestinian Christian community viewed Jesus' death as a good. It was soteriological, an atonement for sins. The interim period between Jesus' Resurrection and parousia was not seen as an inactive waiting period. Rather, this community saw it as the time of Jesus' present rule as Messiah.

After the miracle, Peter had to defend himself before the leaders of the Jews. Luke has him give a speech which contains statements from this second stage's Christology:

> Then, Peter, filled with the Holy Spirit, addressed them: 'Rulers of the people, and elders! If you are questioning us today about an act of kindness to a cripple, and asking us how he was healed, then I am glad to tell you all, and indeed would be glad to tell the whole people of Israel, that it was by the name of Jesus Christ the Nazarene, the one you crucified, whom God raised from the dead, by this name and by no other that this man is able to stand up perfectly healthy, here in your presence, today. This is the stone rejected by you the builders, but which has proved to be the keystone. For of all the names in the world given to man, this is the only one by which we can be saved' (Acts 4:8-12).

Peter quotes from Psalm 118:22. The Jews' "No" to Jesus is corrected by God's "Yes." The "rejected stone" refers to Jesus' death. But God has now made this death into a salvific keystone for men. We are thus in stage two, at which time the Palestinian Christian community viewed Jesus' death as a salvific good planned by God rather than simply the work of evil men. The community sees itself as men saved by the death of Jesus.

The Hellenistic Jews were more familiar with LXX than with MT. They searched the Old Testament for a deeper understanding of the meaning of Christ. The delay of Christ's parousia caused them to move Jesus' reign as the Lord back from His parousia to His exaltation. Later, when His earthly life was seen 'as an epiphany of the Christ, the community would date His reign as the Christ from His baptism. After His exaltation, Jesus now reigns over His community. In the Christology of the Hellenistic Jewish mission, God had sent Jesus to earth. God worked through Him in His earthly ministry; He raised Him from the dead; and He exalted Him at His right hand. There He rules the Church through His Spirit until His parousia.

Peter's discourse in Acts. 2:14-39 contains statements from the Christology of the Hellenistic Jewish mission:

> God raised this man Jesus to life, and all of us are witnesses to that. Now raised to the heights by God's right hand, he has received from the Father the Holy Spirit, who was promised, and what you see and hear is the outpouring of that Spirit. For David himself never went up to heaven; and yet these words are his: 'The Lord said to my Lord: "Sit at my right hand until I make your enemies a footstool for you" ' (Acts. 2:32-35).

Peter quotes Psalm 110:1 which refers to Jesus as "Lord." Just as David assumed the rule of Israel at His enthronement, so Jesus assumed His reign over His community at His exaltation. He sends the Holy Spirit to guide them until all the forces opposing His reign are subdued. For them Jesus is the New David. The Palestinian Jews would have used the MT reading of the psalm. The Hebrew reads: *ne'um*

*YHWH la'donīy.* "The Lord said to my lord." The form *la'donīy* was used for the Davidic king and not as the substitute for Yahweh. Thus it would readily apply to the king of Israel. But the Hellenistic Jews, who used the LXX, would have read the Greek *eipen ho Kyrios tō (i) Kyriō(i) mou.* "The Lord said to my Lord." The LXX text would readily refer the second "Lord" to the Messiah, and would suggest itself to the Hellenistic Jews as a prophecy of the role of Christ at His exaltation.

Thus the Christian community of the Hellenistic Jews saw Jesus becoming the Christ, the new David, at His exaltation to the right hand of the Father. He sends His Spirit to His Church. During His exalted state, He is not inactive. Rather, He rules and guides the community as Lord and Messiah.

Paul's speech in Acts 13:16-41 also contains statements from the Christology of the Hellenistic Jews. Jesus' exaltation parallels and surpasses David's enthronement as king of Israel. In Psalm 2:7 David has been called God's son at His enthronement. The psalm did not mean this to refer to David's *being*. Rather, it referred to his *role:* he acted in the place of God, by ruling over Yahweh's people. He took over the *function* of God in his relationship to the community. But if this was true of the Davidic monarchy, the Hellenistic Jews felt it was even more true of Jesus in His exalted state. The Hellenistic Jews called Jesus the Son of God, but they meant this as a description of His reign over the community. The exalted Christ exercised God's reign over men. The community did not yet attest to Jesus *being* the Son of God. For the Jewish mentality was not interested in *being* but in *activity*. The gentile mission would understand this sonship as revealing *who Jesus is,* while for the Hellenistic Jews it explained *what Jesus is doing right now for them.* Christ assumed the role of reigning over men as David had once assumed the role of reigning over the nation Israel as Yahweh's representative:

> As scripture says in the first psalm:[2] 'You are my son: today I have become your father.' The fact that God raised him from the dead, never to return to corruption, is no more than what he had declared: 'To you I shall give the sure and holy things promised to David.' This is explained by another text: 'You will not allow your holy one to experience corruption.' Now when David in his own time had served God's purposes he died; he was buried with his ancestors and has certainly 'experienced corruption.' The one whom God has raised up, however, has not 'experienced corruption' (Acts. 13:34-37).

In this discourse Luke has Paul yoke together Is. 55:3 and Ps. 16:9 to present the exalted Christ as the New David. The citations form a polemical argument against any interpretation which would apply the texts to David or to the Davidic monarchy. For the Hellenistic Jews these texts are Messianic prophecies. How much better a king is the risen and exalted Christ than David, who died like all other men!

For the Christian community of the Hellenistic Jews the kingdom of God is not equated with the nation of Israel. The kingdom also belongs to those who have assented to subject themselves to the reign of Christ. Thus the kingdom exists both inside of human history as well as outside of it. How does the risen Lord reach those of His followers within human history? Through the Holy Spirit, who

---

[2]Ps. 2 is referred to as "the first psalm," because in the older versions of the Bible both of them were written together.

guides them to do good and to conquer those evil forces still hostile to His reign. This Christian community, aware of its own reception of the power of the Spirit in its own earthly history, begins to comprehend the earthly life of Jesus as the work of the Spirit, too.

This can be seen in parts of Peter's discourse to Cornelius and his household in Acts. 10:34-43. The Christology here also comes from the Hellenistic Jews. God has anointed Jesus (made Him the Christ, "the Anointed") at His baptism. Their own view has moved Jesus' role as the Christ back from His exaltation to His baptism. He works through the Holy Spirit, who makes the earthly life of Jesus an epiphany of His Christ-role. He has the power to subdue the forces of despair while in human history because He has the Holy Spirit.

> God has anointed him with the Holy Spirit and with power, and because God was with him, Jesus went about doing good and curing all who had fallen into the power of the devil (Acts. 10:38).

If Jesus now works in human history through the Spirit, the Hellenistic Jews also realize that this world has now become the stage for the drama between grace and sin, hope and despair. Jesus will not only judge at the end of the world, but even now is judging the actions of men. Later on in this discourse, Peter describes Jesus as exercising the *function* of the divine Judge. This is the insight of the Hellenistic Jews. Later, the gentile mission would understand this role as coming from His divine right as the Son of God. *God has appointed him to judge everyone, alive or dead* (Acts. 10:42).

The gentile mission made the last contribution to the development of the Christology of the first century. They conceived of salvation as a power which could dominate the blind fates which controlled their lives. Thus they were interested in Jesus as the Savior. Paul had not concentrated on the earthly life of Jesus as an epiphany of His role as Savior. But the later gentile mission did. The Son was preexistent; He was incarnated into Jesus; His earthly life was a manifestation of His sonship; and His death was salvific. After His Resurrection, He reigns as the Lord until His parousia. This three-stage Christology of preexistence, incarnate life, and risen glory is Luke's own view. For Luke, the Jesus of history manifests himself as Christ the Savior.

## Luke: His View of Christ and the Christian Community

Luke's own Christology belongs to the Christian community of the gentile mission. Jesus is the Savior; his Christian community has been saved by Him; thus they constitute a people of hope. For Luke the Christian community lives in the third stage of salvation history. In the first stage, the nation Israel had hoped in the coming of the Messianic kingdom. In the second stage, Jesus Christ came as the center of salvation history. He fulfilled the genuine aspirations of Israel. In the third stage, the Christian community proclaims Jesus' salvation to men. The community's mission to the world occurs during the period which stretches from Jesus' initial victory at His Resurrection to His ultimate victory at His parousia. During this in-between time, the Christian community must stay in this world. It must work with a world often hostile to its proclamation of Christ. This world often persecutes the community. Often the members feel tempted to fall victim to despair. Luke insists that the true follower of Christ does not despair. Jesus' inevitable victory over the hostility of the world makes the time of waiting and persecution endurable.[3]

Luke avoids making this final victory of the kingdom a part of human history. He deliberately places the kingdom at a distance from current history. Thus he can treat of Jesus' life as a history of events which has nothing to do with the immediacy of the final day (Conzelmann, p. 119, n. 1). Luke carefully keeps Jesus' work of salvation within the context of human history. He depicts events in the life of Jesus as a preparation for man's redemption, avoiding the connotation that these events prepare for the immediate entrance of the kingdom into human history. Some parts of Mark, on the other hand, would seem to sustain an earlier view. Mark wrote when apocalyptic fervor permeated the Christian community.

These apocalypticists expected the risen Christ to break into human history quite soon. He would conquer all his enemies. The Messianic kingdom, the true nation of Israel, would come upon them. They would enjoy the fruits of the Messianic banquet, and would possess the political power which David's reign once had.

For example, Mark seems to present Christ's glorious entrance into Jerusalem on Palm Sunday as a preparation for the immediate arrival of the kingdom. The people shout assent to Jesus' message. They cry out for the advent of the kingdom. They await the ideal Israel which was symbolized by the rule of David. Mark seems to portray this event as eschatological: the last day is near. (Years later, Luke's community — as we shall see — did not view it in the same light.) His description also has its

---

[3]Hans Conzelmann *The Theology of St. Luke* (New York: Harper and Row, 1960), p. 209. Hereafter cited as: Conzelmann.

political implication: the powers of this world are about to crumble before the onslaught of God's coming kingdom.

> Many people spread their cloaks on the road, others greenery which they had cut in the fields. And those who went in front and those who followed were all shouting: 'Hosanna! Blessings on him who comes in the name of the Lord! Blessings on the coming kingdom of our father David! Hosanna in the highest heavens!' He entered Jerusalem and went into the Temple (Mark 11:8-10).

Luke tones down such apocalyptic fervor in his account of the entrance. He does not have the people acclaim the coming kingdom. Rather, they proclaim *what Jesus had done in the past for them.* Luke does not have Jesus enter the Temple during this acclamation. For his community this entrance would symbolize the end of time and bring to a close all formal worship; for the Messiah himself would take over the reign of human history.

> So they took the colt to Jesus, and throwing their garments over its back they helped Jesus on to it. As he moved off, people spread their cloaks in the road, and now, as he was approaching the downward slope of the Mount of Olives, the whole group of disciples joyfully began to praise God at the top of their voices for all the miracles they had seen. They cried out:
> 'Blessings on the King who comes,
> in the name of the Lord!
> Peace in heaven
> and glory in the highest heavens! (Luke 19:35-38).

Luke deliberately portrays Jesus' entry into Jerusalem at the end of His public ministry as a non-eschatological event.. Further, he presents it as having no political implications whatsoever. Jesus, in Luke, has rejected this political view of His work. He has no intention of setting up the kingdom in Jerusalem (Conzelmann, p. 74). For Luke, the Jesus of history remains cautiously nonpolitical. He does not inspire apocalyptic fervor for the new kingdom. Rather, He carefully prepares His followers to comprehend that His message is one of salvation and not of political power. His followers must stay in history, and come to terms with the powers of history, such as the Roman empire. Luke is saying as much to his own Christian community.

Mark has sayings which state that the kingdom will come with great immediacy. It will soon overpower human history. Men will see the power of God over human history with their own earthly eyes. The kingdom will be a tangible event. It will be something Jesus' hearers will handle and enjoy for themselves. *I tell you most solemnly, there are some standing here who will not see death before they see the kingdom of God come with power* (Mark 9:11). But for Luke, the Christian community which follows Jesus will not experience this concrete event. Rather, they will experience the power of Christ in their lives. After His parousia, *then* the kingdom will be *seen. I tell you truly, there are some standing here who will not taste death before they see the kingdom of God* (Luke 9:27). In this context, the "kingdom" refers to Jesus' work of salvation. Jesus' listeners saw the salvation which came from Christ; they did not see the Messianic kingdom. Thus their experience of the kingdom is one of the effects of salvific grace in their lives. It is not the triumphant kingdom of political power. Thus they had an experience which came from a spiritual vision (or understanding of Christ's salvation) and not from an earthly vision (Conzelmann, p. 114, n. 3).

Paul also saw his own time as the "last days." *Well, now is the favorable time; this is the day of salvation* (II Cor. 6:2). In contrast, Luke views salvation as *already* a past event. The time of salvation has already happened in human history. Jesus' salvation is a special period of time which *does* determine the present. But this salvation itself is over and finished. Luke 22:35-36 clearly distinguishes between the time of Jesus' mission and the present mission of His Christian community in a hostile world. Now the community must arduously prepare itself in order to proclaim Christ. Jesus is no longer within human history to smooth out the rough paths.

> He said to them: 'When I sent you out without purse or haversack or sandals, were you short of anything?' 'No,' they said. He said to them: 'But now if you have a purse, take it; if you have a haversack, do the same; if you have no sword, sell your cloak to buy one.'

The end of time did not come with Jesus. For Luke, Jesus Christ establishes the center of salvation history. He is the end of the history of Israel, the nation of hope. He inaugurates the Christian community, the people of hope. Luke does not see this Christian community waiting upon the coming kingdom of God with apocalyptic fervor. Graced with the salvation which has been gained by Christ, this community now constitutes a people of hope. They work with Christ to prepare the world for His kingdom. Thus, in Luke's eyes, the Christian community can no longer avoid human history. It does not expect an immediate victory over the hostile world by the risen Christ. Rather, this community must stay within history, but change it by being a people of hope. Jesus' life did not reveal what would be coming soon into human history. Rather, He revealed the ultimate future of His community. This ultimate future, His inevitable victory, gives His community sufficient grounds to trust and confide in their own role in salvation history. God guarantees the victory for them, as He still does today for us:

> The meaning of this, however, is simply that the End did not come with Jesus. The truth is that in the life of Jesus in the center of the story of salvation a picture is given of the future time of salvation — a picture that is now the ground of our hope: His life is an event which now procures for us forgiveness and the Spirit, and thereby entrance into a future salvation. Yet this in no way alters the fact that the period of Jesus, like the present, is not yet the End. The good news is not that God's kingdom has come near, but that the life of Jesus provides the foundation for the hope of the future kingdom. Thus the nearness of the kingdom has become a secondary factor (Conzelmann, pp. 36-37).

By its very nature, apocalyptic fervor causes an imminent hope which belongs only to the present. It cannot be handed down by tradition. But the purpose of hope, the concepts of what the community ardently desires, these can be transmitted to others. Thus, in the first century of the Christian community, apocalyptic fervor and patient hope frequently merge into one another. This happens because apocalyptic fervor has to be expressed in concepts. These concepts lay the foundation for a patient hope. Such a hope, however, must itself be grounded in the real world. So patient hope never really loses touch with the apocalyptic desire to secure relief from the powers of this world. Luke used his apocalyptic sources, not so much to abandon the apocalyptic but to make it workable for his contemporaries. Yet time itself had played a vital role in this Lucan transformation. For the delay of the parousia had changed apocalyptic fervor into patient hope for his own community (Conzelmann, p. 97).

In the early days of the Christian community, the apocalypticists eagerly looked forward to a cosmic, universal resurrection which would come quite soon. Luke, instead, concentrates on a corollary of this hope. He emphasizes the resurrection of the *individual* Christian (Conzelmann, p. 110). Luke has Paul proclaim this individual hope before the tribunals of the power of this world. Luke no longer has the Christian feel he will automatically conquer the world simply because he belongs to Christ. There will be a resurrection for the *individual.* This implies a *judgment* will come upon this individual. Therefore each Christian must keep his own conscience ready to meet his judge. The stress is now on personal responsibility rather than on the eventual universal communal victory of the Christians. Paul compares himself with the Jews who believe in the Resurrection and tells his listeners:

> I hold the same hope in God as they do that there will be a resurrection of good men and bad men alike. In these things, I, as much as they, do my best to keep a clear conscience at all times before God and men (Acts. 24:15-16).

Luke stresses the resurrection of the just. This encourages the community of believers to hope. To prevent presumption, however, Luke wants them to realize that they too must face an individual judgment. And to prevent despair, Luke reminds his community of the forgiving nature of their judge (Conzelmann, p. 111, n. 1, See Luke 15).

Luke does not consider the time of this resurrection and judgment as of primary importance. Rather, he wants the Christian community to base its hope not so much on the belief that the kingdom is near, but that it is *inevitable*. This inevitable victory itself validates Jesus' summons to the community to cooperate with Him in the work of salvation. In this way, Luke can retain the fervor of the apocalyptic era. But he turns the community's gaze away from *when* the End will be. He still maintains all the traditional concepts about the coming kingdom. But with his approach, the delay of the parousia no longer challenges the community's faith. For the future event now becomes a future state. It will begin for the Christian at an appointed moment. Even so, it still remains a *fact*, a future reality which calls out to the Christian to so order his life that he can meet it honestly (cf. Conzelmann, p. 111).

Luke does not regard the proper preparation for this coming kingdom to be simply the ardent desire of the whole community. Rather, proper preparation funnels down into the life of the individual Christian. It demands his total allegiance. Each Christian must now become a man of hope in his own personal life. The future is no longer individualized. The community's apocalyptic fervor has now become the individual's need to cooperate with grace. For instance, Luke 16:9-13 stresses the obligation of the individual Christian to cooperate with grace (Conzelmann, pp. 111-112).

The original community of Christians felt obliged to withstand or ignore the power of the state. The state compromised with human history. Salvation came from outside of human history. The state contradicted the coming kingdom. The state had put Jesus to death; it had tried to prevent the king from establishing His kingdom on earth. But Luke regards the events of Christ's life as a part of history. So the Christian community also belongs to human history. Hence Christians must no longer withstand the state. The community must now enter into dialogue with it. Part of this conversation on the part of the Christian community will necessitate that it prove to the Roman empire that neither Christ nor Paul nor the present community constitute a danger to the present political establishment (Conzelmann, p. 138). This explains the apologetic thrust of Luke's Gospel and Acts. Both are at pains to portray Jesus and Paul as nonpolitical figures. But neither man was that removed from the history of his own time.

Luke sees his own age as a secular one. The time of salvation has come and gone. But Luke inspires his Christian community with the courage to withstand the power of this world. This is his good news: the hope of the Christian community depends on Jesus' salvation which had already taken place in redemptive history. From the apocalyptic tradition the community had learned that redemptive history will finally end this world of evil power. So the Christian community, small and powerless at this time, and often the victim of violent persecutions, had the strength to continue to hope in their eventual victory (Conzelmann, p. 196).

Through his view of Christ, therefore, Luke identified the Christian community as a people of hope. They rely on Christ's eventual victory to sustain their hope while they remain in history. They do not expect His immediate return; but they firmly trust in His eventual victory over the evil forces of the world. Thus each Christian becomes a man of hope. So:

as one no longer thinks of oneself as awaiting an imminent parousia, but is aware of a future judgment as an indisputable fact, the figure of Jesus comes to be seen as belonging to past history. Both the parousia and the life of Jesus are connected with the present, but a modification has clearly taken place as regards the early expectation. The connection of the parousia with the present does not consist in the fact that it is near at hand, but in the fact that, whenever it takes place it will be of decisive importance one day in the future for everyone (Conzelmann, p. 186).

## The Story of Pentecost

A close study of Luke's account of the story of Pentecost in Acts 2:1-41 will give us a clearer understanding of his view of the nature of the Christian community.[4]

Before the Hebrew conquest, Pentecost, "the fiftieth day," was a Canaanite festival which celebrated the June wheat harvest. The Israelites took it over and called it "The Feast of the Harvest" (Ex. 23-16). Exodus 34:22 identified it with the Feast of Weeks, but this seems to be a textual gloss yoking together the Canaanite festival with the pilgrimage of weeks referred to in Deut. 18:9-10.

The feast was celebrated seven weeks after the barley harvest (The Feast of the Unleavened Bread). The ritual prescribed in Lev. 23:15-21 sets the celebration on the day after the seventh sabbath of the day of the unleavened bread. This would number 50 days: *pentēkonta hēmeras* in LXX. It is called the Feast of Weeks in II Mac. 12:31-32, while Tob 2:1 terms it *both* The Feasts of Weeks and Pentecost.

Although this feast was one of the three days in the liturgical year at which every male Jew was

---

[4]The following material relies for the most part on Edward Mally, S.J.'s, lectures on "The Acts of the Apostles" at Woodstock-in-New York during Spring, 1970. See also B.F. Meyer "The Meaning of Pentecost," *Worship* Vol. 40 (1966), pp. 281-287 and L. Swain, "Pentecost and the New Covenant," *Clergy Review* vol. 51 (1966), pp. 369-377.

expected to appear before the temple in Jerusalem, it never had much significance for normative Judaism. However, the feast was celebrated 50 days after the Feast of the Unleavened Bread (the Exodus). Exodus 19:1-3 dates the arrival at Sinai on the third new moon after leaving Egypt. Since the 50th day came near this "third moon," later Jewish tradition associated Pentecost with the arrival of the Israelites at Mt. Sinai. Apparently, it had this significance for the early apostles and disciples who were commemorating this secondary feast when an event of great formative spiritual import happened to them — the coming of the Holy Spirit upon the Christian community. In Acts. 2:1 Luke identifies the day as *tēs pentēkostēs*, and describes this coming of the Holy Spirit upon the Christian community as a highly decisive event.

Pentecost was then a commemoration of the time when Moses ascended the mountain of God, witnessed a magnificent theophany, and returned with the Law for the people. Apparently Luke's Pentecostal narrative derives from an earlier Palestinian stratum. In it Jesus was compared to the servant-prophet Moses. In this typology, Moses went up to the holy-mountain-of-God, the people below witnessed a dramatic theophany, and Moses returned with the Law and the new covenant which united all the Hebrews into one people. Luke associates Jesus' Ascension with Moses' going-up-to-the holy-mountain-of-God. Both are accompanied by a cloud (cf Ex. 19:9 with Acts 1:9). In the Palestinian typology Jesus arose, went up to His exaltation at the right hand of God, sent the Holy Spirit accompanied by dramatic theophanies, and gave His community a new law and a new covenant which united them together more firmly.

We can see this more clearly if we study the

traditions associated with the Sinai theophany. Philo and the later rabbis associated "fire," "wind," a "mighty sound," and "tongues" with the theophany. Yet Philo did not mean these external signs to be taken literally. For example, he thought that the "mighty thunder" heard on Mt. Sinai signified that God's voice was so clear that everyone could understand it. Luke also employs these traditional signs of God's theophany. He does not attest to their literal accuracy, but uses them to explain the effectiveness of God's presence in the first community. Luke's own community would recognize these signs as symbols of the effective power of God's coming in grace. All of these signs had ample examples in the Old Testament theophanies which were associated with the self-identity of the nation of hope. Luke uses them to present a self-identity to the Christian community. He associates them with its origin.

Exodus employs the following symbols to describe God's coming to Moses on Mt. Sinai:

> The mountain of Sinai was entirely wrapped in smoke, because Yahweh had descended on it in the form of fire. Like smoke from a furnace the smoke went up, and the whole mountain shook violently. Louder and louder grew the sound of the trumpet. Moses spoke, and God answered him with peals of thunder (Ex. 19:18-19).

Deuteronomy also uses the same technique:

> He let you hear his voice out of heaven for your instruction; on earth he let you see his great fire, and from the heart of the fire you heard his word (Deut. 4:36).

In Acts 2:2 Luke says that the Spirit came "like a powerful wind." He does not claim that the coming of the Spirit *was* a mighty wind, but "like" one. Significantly, he is using a traditional sign of God's theophany to emphasize the effectiveness of His presence. Thunder and fire are also traditional signs of God's coming. (Cf. Is. 66:15, the LXX version, in which God *hōs pūr hēksei kai hōs kataigis*, "like fire he comes, and like thunder.") Mt. Sinai had been filled with the smoke of God's presence, and Luke tells us that the noise of the wind "filled the entire house" (Acts. 2:2).

> When Pentecost day came round, they had all met in one room, when suddenly they heard what sounded like a powerful wind from heaven, the noise of which filled the entire house in which they were sitting; and something appeared to them that seemed like tongues of fire; these separated and came to rest on the head of each of them. They were all filled with the Holy Spirit, and began to speak foreign languages as the Spirit gave them the gift of speech (Acts. 2:1-4).

Luke writes that the theophany "seemed like tongues of fire." Both the passive voice of the verb and the qualifier "like" emphasize that this does not entail the literal appearance of fiery tongues. Rather, Luke's account insists that the recipients of the Spirit had a genuine supernatural experience. This brought about a radical change in their personalities, which was symbolized by using this external sign which revealed God's presence in them. Apparently, the initial effect of this outpouring of the Spirit had been glossolalia, the speaking in unknown tongues mentioned in I Cor. 14:6-12. Instead, Luke has the apostles who receive the Holy Spirit speak in foreign tongues known to the visitors from the Jewish diaspora.

> Now there were devout men living in Jerusalem from every nation under heaven, and at

> this sound they all assembled, each one bewil-
> dered to hear these men speaking his own lan-
> guage. They were amazed and astonished (Acts.
> 2:5-6).

The Jews "assembled" together. Here they form a
unity to hear the proclamation of the apostles about
Jesus. The image suggests the cultic assembly, when
all of the people worship God with one heart. It
recalls the nation of Israel assembled together at the
foot of Mt. Sinai. When Moses spoke to the
assembly:

> Then all the people answered as one: 'All that
> Yahweh has said, we will do' (Ex. 19:8).

Luke begins this theme of universal harmony in
Acts. 2:1 when he describes the first community
gathered together "in one room." Their visible unity
mirrors the unaminity of the Israelites at the foot of
Mt. Sinai when they approved of their covenant
with Yahweh. Later rabbinical tradition would hold
that all of the Jews of all times were present at this
covenantal agreement. All were "of one heart."
Luke is at pains to portray the first Christian community as united in the same way.

The whole episode ends with the dramatic proclamation of the risen Christ to the Jews of the
diaspora. The listing of the nations in Acts. 2:9-11 is
an old oriental form which reflects a Near Easterner's concept of "the whole world." It also
reflects the conviction of the early Palestine Christian community that the Messianic kingdom would
be inaugurated by the universal return of all of the
Jews of the diaspora to the city of Jerusalem.

Jewish apocalypticists expected "The Day of
Yahweh" to come with this union of all the Jews of
the diaspora. The great eschatological event would
be accompanied with the outpouring of God's Spirit
upon His people. These apocalypticists often used

Ezekiel's prophecies to describe that day:

> They will know that I am Yahweh their God,
> when I rescue the captives from the pagans and
> reunite them in their own country, not leaving a
> single one behind. I shall never hide my face
> from them again, since I shall pour out my Spirit
> on the House of Israel — it is the Lord Yahweh
> who speaks (Ez. 39:28-29).

This day would establish a new creation. It would
restore the fruitfulness of the land. It would bring a
blessing on the children of the Jews:

> For I will pour out water on the thirsty soil,
> streams on the dry ground.
> I will pour my spirit on your descendants,
> my blessing on your children (Is. 44:3).

The Spirit would bring dramatic charismatic gifts.
The gentiles would talk in a new speech; they would
be united in the same worship of the same God:

> Yes, I will then give the peoples
> lips that are clean,
> so that all may invoke the name of Yahweh
> and serve him under the same yoke (Zep. 3:9).

Every Jew would enjoy the ability to prophesy on
that day. At one time the Spirit's gift of prophesy
had been limited to one man (I Sam. 10:6) or to a
group of special men favored by God (Num. 11:25).
But on that day, the Spirit would come on *all* the
children of Israel. They would all be able to prophesy (Is. 32:15-18; Joel. 3:1).

Originally, the Jews had conceived of the Day of
Yahweh as a judgment against all the enemies of
Israel. But Amos warned that it would also be a
judgment against the faithless Jews (Am 5:18-20).
Even the nation of God's people would have to face
the divine judgment. All were therefore summoned
to repentance, but only the faithful remnant would
escape destruction, because they had cried out to
the Lord:

They made their hearts adamant rather than listen to the teaching and the words that Yahweh Sabaoth had sent by his spirit through the prophets in the past (Zec. 7:12).

Later Judaism sometimes saw the Day of Yahweh as bringing spiritual gifts, rather than simply the restoration of the nation (cf. Ez. 36:26-28). There would be a new covenant of the Spirit. It would replace the covenant of the law which Jeremiah felt the Jews had lost for good (Jer. 31:32). The Spirit would pour His charismatic gifts on all the Jews of this new covenant. God would bring "peace, genuine peace to those far and near." (Is 57:19, LXX reads: *eirēnēn ep' eirēnē(i) tois makran kai tois eggus ousi.)*

According to Jeremiah, on that day God would transform His people from within. He would be the principle of love and intelligibility within them. He portrays a new Israel. It will be interiorly re-created to know and serve God. Joel also sees the last day as the universal outpouring of the Holy Spirit. The external sign of this outpouring would be the ability of the Jews to prophesy because of their charismatic inspiration.

Luke has Peter employ some of these ideas in his Pentecost sermon. The older Palestinian stratum contains the idea of linking Pentecost with this day of Yahweh; it is an eschatological event. It is an experience of spiritual renewal rather than an apocalyptic restoration of the state of Israel. Luke also adds a later stratum from the gentile mission. The gentile mission, for Luke, is foreshadowed at Pentecost, when the proclamation of Jesus began to go out to people from all over the world. The narrative limits the preaching to Jews, but Luke so arranges his material that he shows the event as decisive for beginning the gentile mission. The earlier Palestinian stratum had already rearranged the eschatological material.

We can understand how this is done if we study how Luke has Peter cite from the prophet Joel, for he adds and deletes from the actual text.

"After this I will pour my Spirit on all mankind. Your sons and daughters shall prophesy, your old men shall dream dreams, and your young men see visions. Even on the slaves, men and women, will I pour out my spirit in those days. I will display portents in heaven and on earth, blood and fire and columns of smoke.

"The sun will be turned into darkness, and the moon into blood, before the day of Yahweh dawns, that great and terrible day. All who call on the name of Yahweh will be saved, for on Mount Zion there will be some who have escaped, as Yahweh has said, and in Jerusalem some survivors whom Yahweh will call" (Joel 3:1-5).

"In the days to come — it is the Lord who speaks — I will pour out my spirit on all mankind. Their sons and daughters shall prophesy, your young men shall see visions, your old men shall dream dreams. Even on my slaves, men and women, in those days, I will pour out my spirit. I will display portents in heaven above and signs on earth below.

"The sun will be turned into darkness and the moon into blood before the great Day of the Lord dawns.

"All who call on the name of the Lord will be saved" (Acts. 2:17-21).

For the Palestinian Christian community Pentecost took on the force of an eschatological event. A later tradition would see the event as a foreboding of the call of the gentiles into the new covenant. Luke's passage has both traditions. Pentecost happens in "the days to come" rather than simply "afterward." This moves the outpouring of the Holy Spirit away from the parousia and brings it into the present situation. Joel has "your" children prophesying. This would limit the charism to the Jewish offspring. But the Lucan parallel has "their" instead, and thus its antecedent is "all mankind." The charism, for Luke, will reach all people. The "the" before the male and female slaves is converted into "my." Joel spoke of the Spirit reaching all classes of Jewish society; even the slaves would enjoy the charism. But Luke changes the sociological class term into a religious one. The slaves are "my" slaves, that is, they belong to God because they have received His Spirit. The Christian community sees itself as a people belonging to God. And this, not because they belong to the nation of Israel, but because they have willingly assented to the work of the Spirit in their hearts.

Luke carefully distinguishes the eschatological signs: there will be *portents* in heaven *above* and *signs* on earth *below*. The term "signs" refers to the words and deeds of Jesus. It also refers to the Pentecostal outpouring of the Spirit. But the portents in heaven are of a different order; they come at the parousia. In this way Luke shows that the Holy Spirit is working right now in the Pentecostal signs rather than putting off His special activity among men until the last day.

This day is "great" for Luke, but not "terrible." Luke sees this present Pentecostal coming of the Spirit as an offering of salvation rather than as a day of judgment. God grants salvation to all who call upon the Lord. For Joel this meant Yahweh, but for

Luke it refers to Jesus. At the end of this prophecy Joel becomes very particular. The salvation to come is for the Jews, for it comes to those on "Mt. Zion" and those "in Jerusalem." Luke avoids this ending so that the "all" who call upon the Lord would not only mean the Jews, but the gentiles also.

The event, for Luke, ends the narrow circle of Jesus' disciples. Now the salvation gained by Jesus is offered to other men too. First to the Jews, and then to the gentiles.

> Hearing this, they were cut to the heart and said to Peter and the apostles: 'What must we do brothers?' 'You must repent,' Peter answered 'and every one of you must be baptized in the name of Jesus Christ for the forgiveness of your sins, and you will receive the gift of the Holy Spirit. The promise that was made is for you and your children, and for all those who are far away, for all those whom the Lord our God will call to himself' (Acts. 2:37-39).

Peter tells his audience that the Messianic days have come, when God offers salvation to all who repent. Jesus has poured out the Holy Spirit (Acts. 2:33). Now the time has come for the audience of Jews to repent. Then, they too, like the apostles, will receive the Holy Spirit. But He is not to be given indiscriminately to all of them, but only to those who repent and accept baptism in Jesus' name as a sign of their repentance. So they will receive what had been promised "for you and your children and for all those who are far away." Originally, those "far away" had referred to the Jews in the diaspora who would return on the last day (Is. 57:19), but now it takes on the connotation of universal salvation. The promise of the Spirit who brings Jesus' salvation to those who repent goes to "all those who are far away," namely, the gentiles. Because they have readily received this salvation, this Christian community of the gentile mission forms a new unity for mankind. It consists of all those -- Jews and gentiles — who have responded to God's summons to cooperate with Him in the work of salvation.

And this is how Luke's own community sees itself: a unified group of men from all over who have assented to God's summons.

## Vatican II's View of Christ and the Self-Identity of the Christian Community

When Pope John XXIII composed a prayer for the success of Vatican II, he had the entire Catholic world plead for a "New Pentecost" to fall upon the Church. The Fathers of Vatican II taught a great deal about Christ and the Christian community in their documents. Here we will explain their teaching within the perspective of the theology of hope. This method will clarify what the theology of hope can contribute to the self-identity of the present-day Christian community. The Spirit comes today to the Christian community and still summons *us* to be a "people of hope."

The Fathers of Vatican II began their Christology with the traditional trinitarian theology. Jesus is the incarnate Son. His Incarnation is a mystery of God. This mystery sheds light on the mystery of man. Christ is the last man in the sense that He is the first man to reach the last day. So He definitively reveals the mystery of the Father to man. He concretizes for each man the Father's love. In turn this divine love reveals man to man. It makes each man aware of his own identity. In Christ, a man can comprehend the supreme summons given to him that he should serve God by loving other men. This divine love gives the Christian community its true self-identity.

The truth is that only in the mystery of the incarnate Word does the mystery of man take on light. For Adam, the first man, was a figure of him who was to come, namely, Christ, the Lord. Christ, the final Adam, by the revelation of the mystery of the Father and his love, fully reveals man to man himself and makes his supreme calling clear. (*Constitution on the Church in the Modern World*, no. 22).

Christ is the visible sign to man of what the invisible God is like. He is the historical manifestation of what the future of God is to be like. So He is the perfect Man; He restores man to his future. This same future Adam had lost by falling victim to history. He fell victim, rather than mastering time as he has been created to do. And Adam made all of his sons and daughters fall victim to time. When Christ became man, He did not annul human nature, but assumed it. So all of us who share in His human nature have been raised to this divine dignity too. Through Mary, Christ was born into history. Through the Father, He has conquered that history. So He is free of that sin which binds man as a victim to time.

He who is 'the image of the invisible God' is himself the perfect man. To the sons of Adam he restores the divine likeness which had been disfigured from the first sin onward. Since human nature as he assumed it was not annulled, by that very fact it has been raised up to a divine dignity in our respect too. For by his incarnation the Son of God has united himself in some fashion with every man. He worked with human hands, he thought with a human mind, acted by human choice, and loved with a human heart. Born of the Virgin Mary, he has truly been made one of us, like us in all things except sin (*Consti-*

*tution on the Church in the Modern World,* no. 22).

The one Man free of history's sin chose to fall victim to it. By this free sacrifice, He gained for all of us the freedom from history which our first parents vainly sought. It is the true freedom from history which does not abstract us from the world. Rather, it reconciles us to the Father and to each other. The devil and sin, the twin forces of despair, are conquered by the Man of hope. Each of us can exclaim in the fullness of God's hope: "God so loved me He sent His Son to save me." Jesus' suffering offers us an example for our imitation. He showed us the way. If we follow His way, our life and our death are no longer meaningless. They are filled with meaning because they are signs of hope.

> As an innocent lamb he merited life for us by the free shedding of his own blood. In him God reconciled us to himself and among ourselves. From bondage to the devil and sin, he delivered us, so that each one of us can say with the apostle: The Son of God 'loved me and gave himself up for me.' By suffering for us he not only provided us with an example for our imitation. He blazed a trail, and if we follow it, life and death are made holy and take on a new meaning. (*Constitution on the Church in the Modern World,* no. 22).

Man is a mystery. Take Christ out of that mystery, and we have a tale of great despair. Christian revelation sees the mystery of man as very great. For man is so very great that Christ has been sent to remove the despair of sorrow and death which hangs over man like the sword of Damocles.

Filled with the new life of hope which comes to us from Christ's victory, each member of the Christian community sees himself as a living member of

God's family. He has God for a Father, Christ as his oldest brother, and he is filled with the love of the Holy Spirit. This Holy Spirit, the future of God now present within each of us, makes us able to leap out of time and call upon God as our Father. For the Spirit brings us to God's future when we will all belong to His family:

> Such is the mystery of man, and it is a great one, as seen by believers in the light of Christian revelation. Through Christ and in Christ, the riddles of sorrow and death grow meaningful. Apart from his Gospel, they overwhelm us. Christ has risen, destroying death by his death. He has lavished life upon us so that, as sons in the Son, we can cry out in the Spirit: Abba, Father! (*Constitution on the Church in the Modern World*, no. 22).

Now the Christian community are those who believe in the risen Christ. They are filled with hope. They have so much hope that they can believe in a world community of universal brotherhood. They do not see this as an "impossible dream." Yet at the same time, Christ warns His followers that their love cannot be just for universal and grandiose abstractions. It must be performed in everyday life with everyday people.

> To those, therefore, who believe in divine love, he gives assurance that the way of love lies open to all men and that the effort to establish a universal brotherhood is not a hopeless one. He cautions them at the same time that this love is not something to be reserved for important matters, but must be pursued chiefly in the ordinary circumstances of life (*Constitution on the Church in the Modern World*, no. 38).

Mary led a very ordinary life. She was a housewife and a mother. But this very ordinary life became for all of us the means of salvation. She is the one who brought Christ into the world. And Christ freed us from history's sin. Mary too has already been raised into the future of God. Her Assumption has made her a sign in this present world of *what the whole Church will be in the future*. She is the first flower to bloom from Christ's salvation. She is the sign of the perfect Church, the Church to be in the world to come. She is a shining star to mankind right now. She is a symbol of hope and a solace for all of her sons and daughters who remain in pilgrimage in history as they strive for God's future. So she is both the first woman to be redeemed by Christ, and the last woman, for she too has been taken into the last day.

In the bodily and spiritual glory which she possesses in heaven, the Mother of Jesus continues in this present world as the image and the first flowering of the Church as she is to be perfected in the world to come. Likewise, Mary shines forth on earth, until the day of the Lord shall come, as a sign of sure hope and solace for the pilgrim People of God (*Constitution on the Church*, no. 68).

Who are the pilgrim People of God? This leads us to consider the self-identity of the Christian and the Christian community. The Christian community is a group of people conformed to Christ. Christ has indicated that we all must play our own role in history. We must be willing to face the pain and the limitations of being human. We must realize we are in combat as we struggle for peace and justice. Christ has been raised to the future of God. His power comes to us from that future through the energy of the Holy Spirit. Christ awakens in us an ardent desire for the world's future. This ardent desire does not take any of us out of history.

Rather, it makes us all the more enthusiastic to make the world more human. We want to submit all of the earth to this future of God.

Undergoing death itself for all of us sinners, he taught us by example that we too must shoulder that cross which the world and the flesh inflict on those who search after peace and justice. Appointed Lord by his resurrection and given plenary power in heaven and on earth, Christ is now at work in the hearts of men through the energy of his Spirit. He arouses not only a desire for the age to come, but, by that very fact, he animates, purifies, and strengthens those noble longings too by which the human family strives to make its life more human and to render the whole earth submissive to this goal (*Constitution on the Church in the Modern World*, no. 38).

Who is the Christian so inspired to do this? Christ has been made the firstborn of the risen dead. The Christian receives from this risen Lord "the first fruits of the Spirit." These Spirit-gifts make him capable of loving in a whole new way. He becomes an agent of the New Law of love. The Spirit is the pledge of his future with God. This future comes into his present, through grace, to renew the whole man right now. Even his physical body participates in this renewal. The Christian cannot lose his future with God, because he cannot die. He is one with the risen Christ who has conquered death.

The Christian man, conformed to the likeness of that Son who is the firstborn of many brothers, receives 'the first fruits of the Spirit' by which he becomes capable of discharging the new law of love. Through this Spirit, who is 'the pledge of our inheritance,' the whole man is renewed from within, even to the achievement of the 'redemption of the body': 'If the Spirit of him who raised Jesus from the dead dwells in you, then he who raised Jesus Christ from the dead will also bring to life your mortal bodies because of his Spirit who dwells in you.' (Rom. 8:11) (*Constitution on the Church in the Modern World*, no. 22).

The Christian does not leave history. His need to do battle with the forces of despair continues. But he has become one with the paschal mystery of Christ. Christ has passed from death through His Resurrection to the Father's future. So the Christian passes from a life of despair through grace to the future of eternal life with God. He lives in history through hope in this future.

Pressing upon the Christian, to be sure, are the need and the duty to battle against evil through manifold tribulations and even to suffer death. But, linked with the paschal mystery and patterned on the dying Christ, he will hasten forward to resurrection in the strength which comes from hope (*Constitution on the Church in the Modern World*, no. 22).

What does the Christian community think of those who surround it? Does it want to withdraw from all the other people in the world working in history? Or does it want to join forces with them? The Christian community can be attracted to joining others. It wants to see an intrinsic attractiveness in these others. It wants to see them really disposed to helping others. It expects that the young will be drawn to those communities which offer them life and hope. It demands the same things of itself.

If every citizen is to feel inclined to take part in the activities of the various groups which make up the social body, these must offer advantages which will attract members and dispose them to serve others. We can justly consider that the future of humanity lies in the hands of those who are strong enough to provide coming generations with reasons for living and hoping (*Constitution on the Church in the Modern World*, no. 31).

## Vatican II: The Christian Community and Its Relationship with Other Men

The joys and the hopes, the griefs and the anxieties of the men of this age, especially those who are poor or in any way afflicted, these too are the joys and hopes, the griefs and anxieties of the followers of Christ. Indeed, nothing genuinely human fails to raise an echo in their hearts. For theirs is a community composed of men. United in Christ, they are led by the Holy Spirit in their journey to the kingdom of their Father and they have welcomed the news of salvation which is meant for every man. That is why this community realizes that it is truly and intimately linked with mankind and its history (*Constitution on the Church in the Modern World*, no. 1).

God summons the people of hope from out of the whole community of men. These Christians are never totally separate from other men. They did not forfeit their humanity by responding to God's summons. Christians can really only cooperate with God's summons to build a mutual future with Him by being true to what they are: by being men. Yet Christians surely do possess a certain uniqueness. Other men do not regard them merely as other humanists. Within the world community of men, Christians stand out in a special way. They are a sign to other men of what the future can be. They alone have staked their whole future on the future of Jesus Christ. Each Christian expects Jesus to be the future of his own personal self. Also, the entire body of Christians expects Jesus to be the future of their whole community. They work in the world for the future of God. And the future of God for them is intimately linked with the future of the risen Jesus. Only by being loyal to His hope for the coming kingdom do Christians expect that they can secure any victory over the forces of despair. Mankind is plagued by these diabolical forces. They seek to disintegrate the human community. They attack the integrity of each man's personality. The people of hope strive to reintegrate each man's personality. They strive to achieve a true world community of men.

How do Christians look at other men? The Christian community does not expect other men to simply lose their future. Christians are not preparing for the new world in order that they can keep it only for themselves. Christians accept the divine will: all men have a mutual future, both in this world and in the kingdom to come. God offers His future to all. Christians stand out for recognizing and cooperating with His summons. But they also recognize that they have other partners in this enterprise. *Anyone who is not against you is for you* (Luke 9:50). In a sense, Christians recognize only two types of men. There are the men who are building the foundations for the coming kingdom of God. And there are others who are vainly striving to prevent its coming.

According to the Fathers of Vatican II, Christians try to demonstrate to other men that their cooperation with God's future does not lessen their human dignity. Rather, their hope in a divine power outside of human history, which is coming toward men, grounds each man's sense of his individual worth. This Christian hope affirms the personal summons from God to each individual. This affirmation requires the belief that each man enjoys the spark of intelligence and his own personal freedom. This intelligence and freedom constitute each man's own dignity. Such a dignity further demands that a society appreciate the unique worth of each of its members. So Christian hope really enhances human dignity.

Christians understand that God calls each man to be His son. He summons each man to communion with Him. God wants each man to share in the happiness of God's future. The Christian community hopes in the coming of God at the end of time. But this hope does not diminish the importance of man's work on this earth. Rather, it gives man a special incentive to perform his tasks more properly. The Christian community realizes that when any man loses touch with this divine summons and this hope in the coming kingdom, then his appreciation of human dignity begins to disintegrate. Modern news media have made all of us grimly aware of how much this loss of the sense of the dignity of the human person plagues the world. It has led to serious crimes and fruitless wars. Such indignities corrupt the human spirit. Christians note that once hope is taken away from man, he can no longer grapple successfully with the forces of human corruption. He is completely puzzled by the riddles of life and death. He yields to guilt and grief. He weakly accepts a bleak despair as his lot.

The Church holds that the recognition of God is in no way hostile to man's dignity, since this dignity is rooted and perfected in God. For man was made an intelligent and free member of society by the God who created him. Even more importantly, man is called as a son to commune with God and share in his happiness. She further teaches that a hope related to the end of time does not diminish the importance of intervening duties, but rather undergirds the acquittal of them with fresh incentives. By contrast, when a divine substructure and the hope of life eternal are wanting, man's dignity is more grievously lacerated, as current events often attest. The riddles of life and death, of guilt and of grief go unsolved, with the frequent result that men succumb to despair (*Constitution on the Church in the Modern World*, no. 21).

Christ has risen into the future of God. He has risen not only for Christians, but for all men. His future with God calls out to all who have come from the creative hand of God. Christians are not the only ones who benefit from Christ's victory of hope. All men who share in the hope of God's future constitute a people of good will. God's grace can work in them because, in some way, they have all responded to His summons. Christ died for all men. All men are summoned to the same future: God's. Christians therefore believe that the Holy Spirit — often in ways which they have no means of detecting — offers to every man the opportunity of being associated with the Man of hope's victory over the forces of despair.

The Word was the true light
that enlightens all men (John 1:9).

Thus the world has the potential to become one community, for all men share in the same hope. The task before Christians is to work with God at building this world into a real community of hope. It should not remain a cluster of isolated islands.

All this holds true not only for Christians, but

for all men of good will in whose hearts grace works in an unseen way. For, since Christ died for all men, and since the ultimate vocation of man is in fact one, and divine, we ought to believe that the Holy Spirit in a manner known only to God offers to every man the possibility of being associated with this paschal mystery (*Constitution on the Church in the Modern World*, no. 22).

Each Christian must heed the warning that he gains nothing by possessing all the power of this world if he has no share in the future of God. Such a man has lost himself, for he has gained everything except the kingdom. And this kingdom will come with such force that it will sweep away all that is not part of its hope. Christians cannot weaken their ardent expectation for a new earth. Yet their hope for the kingdom does not debilitate their concern for this world. Rather, it fires them with a genuine concern for cultivating this world. For on the soil of this earth God has planted the seed of the new human family. Here on this earth men of hope can discern the intimations of the future age.

Therefore, while we are warned that it profits a man nothing if he gain the whole world and lose himself, the expectation of a new earth must not weaken but rather stimulate our concern for cultivating this one. For here grows the body of a new human family, a body which even now is able to give some kind of foreshadowing of the new age (*Constitution on the Church in the Modern World*, no. 39).

Christians realize that there is a real distinction between the progress of this world and the growth of Christ's kingdom. But that genuine progress which enhances the human spirit does contribute to the better ordering of human society. This vitally concerns the kingdom of God, for the future of God's reign reaches out to all men who now cooperate with the coming Lord.

Earthly progress must be carefully distinguished from the growth of Christ's kingdom. Nevertheless, to the extent that the former can contribute to the better ordering of human society, it is of vital concern to the kingdom of God (*Constitution on the Church in the Modern World*, no. 39).

But Christians do not totally identify themselves with a secular humanism which feels man has complete control over the coming kingdom. Even as Christians work and sweat to build the kingdom on earth, they realize that all depends on God. Scripture has taught them that the man who builds a house without a solid foundation (hope in God) will lose it. And a society which builds a civilization without God will eventually crumble.

But everyone who listens to these words of mine and does not act on them will be like a stupid man who built his house on sand. Rain came down, floods rose, gales blew and struck that house, and it fell; and what a fall it had! (Matt. 7:26-27).

If Yahweh does not build the house,
  in vain the masons toil;
If Yahweh does not guard the city,
  in vain the sentries watch (Ps. 127:1).

Thinking that they have found serenity in an interpretation of reality everywhere proposed these days, many look forward to a genuine and total emancipation of humanity wrought solely by human effort. They are convinced that the future role of man over the earth will satisfy every desire of his heart (*Constitution on the Church in the Modern World*, no. 10).

233

Christians also build for this new world. But they are the community of hope. So they realize that when all the plans are done, God will still be summoning them to "something new." They can never be satisfied completely with this world, no matter how renewed it becomes, until God comes to take it into His future. They remain a pilgrim people of hope until God's kingdom comes.

Amen: come, Lord Jesus (Rev. 22:20).

# BIBLIOGRAPHY

## Books

Albright, William Foxwell. *From Stone Age to Christianity*. Baltimore: Johns Hopkins, 1940.

Alves, Rubem A. *A Theology of Human Hope*. Washington: Corpus Books, 1969.

Benoit, O.P., Pierre. *The Passion and Resurrection of Jesus*. New York: Herder and Herder, 1969.

Bloch, Ernst. *Das Prinzip Hoffnung*. Frankfurt: Suhrkamp, 1959.

Bornkamm, Günther. *Jesus of Nazareth*. New York: Harper and Row, 1960.

Bultmann, Rudolf (and Karl Kundsin). *Form Criticism*. New York: Harper Torch book, 1962.

*The History of the Synoptic Tradition*. New York: Harper and Row, 1963.

Conzelmann, Hans. *The Theology of St. Luke*. New York: Harper and Row, 1960.

Cox, Harvey. *The Feast of Fools*. Cambridge: Harvard University Press, 1969.

*Dewart, Leslie. The Future of Belief: Theism in a World Come of Age*. New York: Herder and Herder, 1966.

Dibelius, Martin. *From Tradition to Gospel.* London: Nicholson and Watson, 1934.

*Documents of Vatican II.* Ed. Walter M. Abbott, S.J. New York: America Press, 1966.

Driver, S. R. *The Book of Exodus.* Cambridge: University Press, 1918.

Fuller, Reginald. *The Foundations of New Testament Christology.* New York: Scribner, 1965.

*The Future of Hope: Theology as Eschatology.* Ed. Frederick Herzog. New York: Herder and Herder, 1970.

*The Human Reality of Sacred Scriptures.* Vol. X. Concilium Series. Eds. Pierre Benoit, O.P. and Roland Murphy, O.Carm. New York: Paulist Press, 1965.

*The Jerome Biblical Commentary.* Eds. Raymond E. Brown, S.S., Joseph A. Fitzmyer, S.J., and Roland E. Murphy, O.Carm. Englewood Cliffs, N.J.: Prentice Hall, 1968.

*The Jerusalem Bible.* Ed. Alexander Jones. Garden City, N.Y.: Doubleday and Company, 1966.

Kaiser, Otto and Kümmel, Werner George. *Exegetical Method: A Student Handbook.* New York: Seabury Press, 1967.

Käsemann, Ernst. *Essays on New Testament Themes.* Napperville, Ill.: A. Allenson, 1964.

Kierkegaard, Sören. *A Kierkegaard Anthology.* Ed. Robert Bretall. New York: The Modern Library, 1959.

McLuhan, Marshall and Fiore, Quentin. *The Medium is the Massage.* New York: Bantam Books, 1967.
　　*Understanding Media.* New York: Signet, 1964.

McNeile, A. H. *The Book of Exodus.* London: Methuen, 1931.

Marxsen, Willi. *Mark the Evangelist.* New York: Abington Press, 1969.

Moltmann, Jürgen. *Theologie der Hoffnung.* Munich: Chr. Kaiser Verlag, 1965. ET *The Theology of Hope.* trans. James W. Leitch. New York: Harper and Row, 1967.

Noth, M. *Exodus: A Commentary.* Philadelphia: Westminster Press, 1962.

Ong, S.J., Walter. *The Presence of the Word.* New Haven: Yale University Press, 1967.

*The Oxford Annotated Bible with the Apocrypha.* Eds. Bruce M. Metzger and Herbert G. May. New York: Oxford University Press, 1962.

Robinson, H. Wheeler. *The Christian Doctrine of Man.* Edinburgh: T. & T. Clark, 1934.

Rohde, Joachim. *Rediscovering the Teaching of the Evangelists.* London: D. M. Barton, 1968.

Russell, D. S. *The Method and Message of Jewish Apocalyptic.* Philadelphia: Westminster Press, 1964.

Schweitzer, Albert. *The Quest of the Historical Jesus.* New York: Macmillan, 1922.

Tödt, Heinz Eduard. *The Son of Man in the Synoptic Tradition.* Philadelphia: Westminster Press, 1965.

von Rad, Gerhard. *Genesis: A Commentary.* trans. John Marks. Philadelphia: Westminster Press, 1961.

Wrede, William. *Das Meissiasgeheimnis in den Evangelien. Zugleich ein Beitrag zum Verständis des Markusevangeliums* Göttingen: 1901.

## Articles

"Christ Jesus: Our Hope." Eds. James Walsh, S.J. and William Yeomans, S.J. *The Way.* VIII. 4 (October, 1968), 251-305.

Cross, Jr., Frank Moore. "Yahweh and the God of the Patriarchs." *Harvard Theological Review.* LV. (1962), 225-259.

"Hope: A Symposium." Ed. Walter N. Capps, *Cross Currents.* XVIII. 3 (Summer, 1968), 257-335.

Käsemann, Ernst. "Beginnings of Christian Theology." *Apocalypticism, Journal for Theology and the Church.* VI. Ed. R. W. Funk, New York: Herder and Herder, 1969.

Meyer, B. F. "The Meaning of Pentecost." *Worship* XL (1966), 281-287.

Sarno, S.J., Ronald A. "Rebuilding the Temple." *The Bible Today.* (February, 1969), 2799-2804.

"The Word of God and the Mass Media." *Chicago Studies.* VII, (Spring, 1968), 15-26.

Stern, Karl. "Thoughts on the Resurrection." *The Catholic Worker.* XXXVI. 2 (February, 1970), 2f.

Swain, L. "Pentecost and the New Covenant." *Clergy Review.* LI. (1966), 369-377).

# Old Testament Index

# New Testament Index

# Author and Subject Index

25 - 101